Journey With Jesus

Books 1-4

Journey With Jesus,

Visions, Dreams, Meditations & Reflections

Journey With Jesus Two,

Silent Prayer and Meditation

Journey With Jesus Three,

How to Avoid the Pitfalls of Spiritual Leadership

Journey With Jesus Four,

The Power of The Gospel

Yong Hui V. McDonald

Journey With Jesus Books 1-4

Transformation Project Prison Ministry
P.O. Box 220
Brighton, CO 80601
www.tppmonline.org

Published by Adora Productions.
Printed in the United States of America
ISBN: 978-1-935791-53-9
First Printing: October 2015

Cover Design: Lynette McClain
McClain Productions, www.mcclainproductions
Cover Drawings and Illustrations: Charles Polk, Alaina Mangeri Gobb, Mario Muñoz, Mannie D. Serna, Holly Weipz, Anthony Perez

DEDICATION

I dedicate this book to our Heavenly Father, our Lord Jesus, the Holy Spirit, and all the people who have the desire to understand God's love and want to learn how to be effective leaders for His kingdom.

ACKNOWLEDGMENTS

I thank God for my wonderful mother, for her love and prayers for me. She prays for me and my ministry day and night. I believe because of her prayers God has blessed me and my ministry beyond my imagination.

My gratitude to all the following generous people who helped with this book: Holly Weipz, Mario Muñoz, Anthony Perez, and Lynette for beautiful cover drawings; Charles Polks, Alaina Mangeri Gobb, Mario Muñoz, Mannie D. Serna, Anthony Perez, Holly Weipz for illustrations; and the following people for editing of the book: Deann L. Anderson, Daun Ayala, , Rudi Duran, Regina Fernandez, Shin Fierke, Rita Finney, Amanda Giron, Kathy Grauer, Gregg Griego, Justin Haubrich, Lori Hill, Amber James, Sister Maureen Kehoe, Laura Nokes Lang, Scott Lorman, Devontae Mason, Maxine Morarie, Douglas Purdy, Heather Robinson, Sam Rodriguez, Tina Sandoval, Erika Simental, Helen Sirios, Charles Slabaugh, Demetrius Trujillo, Bruce Uchida. Helen Hollon, Deborah Stubbs, Elisha Ostnuger, Sharon Gallegos, Danielle Christensen, Stephanie Quezada, Jasminh Campbell, Carol Emery, Christopher Wade, Young Ja Chang and Alicia Lewis-Jackson.

I especially thank Charles Polk, Mario Muñoz and Anthony Perez who drew most of all the illustrations. They did a great job and Holly edited some of their drawings. In addition, I would like to express my sincere thanks to Douglas Purdy and Rita Finney who did an excellent job of editing of all four *Journey With Jesus* and many other books. Thank you all for your hard work and dedication to serve the Lord.

Finally, I give glory to Jesus. Without him, this book couldn't have been written.

CONTENTS

Journey With Jesus Two, Silent Prayer and Meditation / 89

Appendices

Journey With Jesus
Visions, Dreams, Meditations, and Reflections

Yong Hui V. McDonald

INTRODUCTION

When God called me to preach in 1997, I told Him that I had no desire to go into the ministry, but I would write a book to help others. I wrote *Moment By Moment I Choose to Love You* in January 1998. I thought I was done with God's work when I finished the book, but the day I finished it I heard clearly the voice of God: "Go and tell them that Jesus died for them and they are forgiven." I still wasn't ready to obey my calling.

God soon called me to pray for ten percent of my time every day, so I started spending time in prayer. Whenever I went to pray, I wept, because God kept calling me to the ministry but I didn't have the heart to follow His call. This lasted about a year.

During these times of struggle, God asked me to read out loud one gospel a day for a year. I obeyed His instruction for many months and learned how much I didn't know about Jesus. Even though I've believed in God all my life, I didn't have a close relationship with Jesus and that was one of the reasons why I had a difficult time obeying God. Eventually this knowledge about Jesus changed the course of my life forever.

One day I started writing, attempting to understand how Jesus speaks to and walks with me. Some ideas in the story originated from visions, dreams, reflections, and meditations, while others grew from an understanding of Jesus. I believe the images, visions, dreams, and understandings I have described originated from God for several reasons.

First, I am not a creative person who imagines anything different from ordinary life. Therefore, there was no way I could have written or thought of an allegorical story.

Second, these images and visions came to my mind after I started spending time in prayer and meditation. I had never experienced this kind of imagery before I made a commitment to spend time with God in prayer.

Third, when the images and visions came to my mind, they always came along with a deep conviction in my heart, as if God were there and speaking to me. I am not saying this to promote or give credibility to my story. God should get all the glory.

Writing *Journey With Jesus* deepened my faith in Jesus. From the start, I was amazed at how much I was able to experience the leading hands of Jesus. I felt so blessed while I was writing the story. I was experiencing Jesus.

Writing about my walk with Jesus was a time of reflection and enlightenment for me as I began to understand how Jesus took care of me through my struggles and difficult times. The process of writing the story helped me to evaluate my commitment to God. Eventually, it helped me to make the decision to start the ordination process and pursue a seminary education at the Iliff School of Theology in order to serve God better in the future.

That was ironic, as my intention in writing the story had been to understand how Jesus had walked with me. Somehow the story led me in a direction I had never intended to go.

I shared *Journey With Jesus story* with others according to God's leading. As time passed, I felt God asking me to share the story with as many as possible. I ignored this request for a while, and when God spoke to me again about this, I asked God, "Why?" I didn't have any desire to make it into a book because the story was personal.

"That story is not yours to keep," God spoke to my heart. "I gave you that story so you could share it with others. It is the story of how I pulled you out of a pit."

"What pit are you talking about, Lord?" I asked with

surprise. God gave me an image in my mind. At the bottom of a deep, dry well there laid a lifeless little doll. God's big hands pulled the doll out of the well. Holding the doll in the palms of his hands, God breathed life into it. The doll transformed into a little girl, full of life.

Then God spoke to my heart, "You were like that doll, lifeless, but I gave you life."

I understood then that it was Jesus who pulled me out of a pit and gave me life. My heart was filled with gratitude and tears came to my eyes. I knew no one in the world would care for me as Jesus does.

Part One:
Journey With Jesus

1. Walking With Jesus

One day, I arrived at church around 5:00 a.m. I sang hymns and asked God what I should read, and He told me Hosea. I finished reading Hosea and some parts of the gospel of Mark, and then I thought it was time to listen to Jesus. I wanted to understand how Jesus walked with me. This meditation continued for many mornings, and it helped me to understand my relationship with Jesus from a new perspective.

I listened to the hymn "How Great Thou Art" and closed my eyes, imagining that I was walking through the woods with Jesus. I didn't expect what I would see next in my mind. I saw a little girl wearing bright white clothes with no seams, holding Jesus' hand. Jesus was also wearing a white robe. The girl looked seven or eight years old and was dancing, jumping, and bounding delightfully. There was tranquility and peace in that green forest. It was a sunny day with a gentle breeze. Everything seemed perfect in that picture. The girl sang hymns about Jesus, who looked more pleased than ever. The birds sang along with the girl. I knew the girl I was seeing in my mind was me.

That wonderful picture didn't last long. The roads got rougher and rougher. Soon she was walking on a road through thorn bushes. Everywhere she turned, there were plants with thorns poking at her. Her dress was dirty and spotted with blood. She didn't understand how she had let go of Jesus'

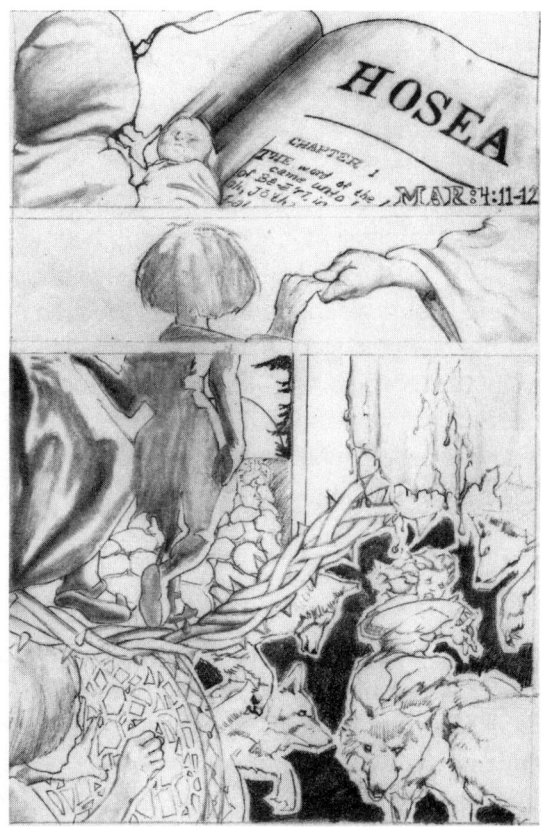

hand. She felt cold, hungry, and lonely. It was getting dark. She was frightened by the howls of a pack of wolves. Her heart raced with fear as she walked and walked.

Exhausted, she fell to the ground and drifted into a deep slumber. In her dreams, a wolf attacked her mother again and again. An unbreakable glass window stood between her and her mother. The girl pounded the glass and screamed for help, but no one came. When she finally saw some people in the distance, she desperately called for help. They didn't pay any attention to her and quickly disappeared.

"Jesus, where are you? If you are out there please come and help me." Someone woke her up. It was Jesus. She heard his voice calling her name and felt relieved. He stretched out his warm, gentle hands and led the way in the moonlight. When she got too tired to walk, Jesus carried her in his arms until they found a stream.

The sun rose and Jesus gently washed her feet. His eyes were full of compassion, and as he wiped her tears, he wept. When his tears touched her clothes, they became clean—the bloodstains disappeared. Jesus touched her wounds and her bleeding stopped; she felt no pain. She was convinced that Jesus could heal. He gave her some bread, and she ate. She felt safe and had peace in her heart.

He held her hands in his and told her lovingly, "Remember to always hold on to my hands. I love you so much. I want you to walk with me."

2. The Thorn Bushes

The girl cried. "I'm terrified every night, Lord. I don't know why my father gets drunk and beats my mother. How I wish I could help her. Can you make my father stop drinking? I know if he quit drinking, he wouldn't hurt my mother."

"He makes his own decision. I tried to tell your father, but he wouldn't listen."

"I didn't know what was happening. I thought I would never get out of the thorns. What was that all about? Did I take the wrong road?"

Jesus said, "It was the road that you had to follow. Everyone goes through periods of suffering. Sometimes people go through these periods longer than others."

"Jesus, why do people have to walk those roads?"

"Actually, people walk through them because they live in the Fallen World. As you walk along the roads, there are many obstacles, thorns, and poisonous snakes. I once lived like you, so I know what you are going through. The best thing about suffering is that it helps people to understand how others are

going through suffering too. It helps people learn how to help other people."

"Did you have to suffer, too?" the girl asked, noticing nail marks in Jesus' hands. She touched the holes gently with her fingers. The holes felt bigger than they looked.

"My beloved child, I have suffered and died for you and other people, so even though people suffer in this life, they don't have to suffer in the next life. Walk close to me and hold on to my hand. I will help you get to our eternal home safely."

Jesus took her hand and started down the road, a road covered with thorn bushes and thistles. Once more she dreamed about her mother being attacked by a wolf again and again. She felt as if she were living in two different worlds. She walked with Jesus during the day, but at night in her dreams she was horrified and alone.

3. The Flowers

One day as they walked along, a group of girls came out and danced, holding flowers in their hands. The girl looked at Jesus and said, "Look at those girls. They have beautiful flowers. I want to have some. I don't know where to get any."

Jesus replied gently, "Those girls have them because their parents gave them the flowers. Their parents are able to provide love, security, and other necessary things for them."

The girl became sad. "I wish I could have flowers like they do. Jesus, it seems they all have some, but I don't. You heard one of the other girls teasing me that I wear crummy clothes."

"Child, I know you don't have what they have. No one gave you any flowers, but I will give you some when we arrive at a flower garden."

She looked at Jesus' face, encouraged. "Really? You will give me flowers?"

"Yes. We have to get to the place where you can pick the ones that you like. Remember, the flowers you will receive in this life are temporary, but the ones I will give you when we get to our Father's home are permanent and more beautiful."

The girl felt better. She smiled and skipped with joy as she walked along. She couldn't help but see the other girls' flowers again. How she wished she could have them. She met some friendly girls who asked her to play with them. She was delighted and quickly let go of Jesus' hand. She ran to play with them.

As she danced with the others, the girl asked, "Do you know who Jesus is?"

"We don't know who Jesus is."

The girl couldn't understand why they didn't know Jesus. One of the girls teased her as they were playing on the playground, "You don't have what we have. You cannot be like us. You don't even have any flowers."

Humiliated, the girl ran to hide from them. She sobbed as she walked along the road. When she was alone, she cried loud and long. The girl knew what she had to do. She was determined to find some flowers for herself. As she wandered around in the forest, she was glad to see wildflowers. When she stretched out her hands to pick them, a snake came out from behind the bush and bit her little finger. She felt a sharp pain. Screaming in terror, she raced to get away from that place. She kept running into the thorn bushes, but didn't care. Her hands and arms became stiff. It was as if she were dying; she felt danger all around her. She knew something bad had happened as she was walking through the valley of the shadow of death. Something had gone totally wrong. She

learned that her younger sister, who became lost and wandered around the thorn bushes, was attacked by a pack of wolves. The wolves crushed her sister into the ground and she died alone.

Overwhelmed with sorrow, the girl cried and cried for her beloved sister. She lost consciousness as the snake poison spread through her body, In her dream, she mourned and dreamed about her sister. Snakes attacked her in her dream. Something was choking her and she struggled to wake up, but she just couldn't. She cried, "Jesus, help me. I need help."

4. The Love of Jesus

When she woke up, Jesus, with love in his eyes, was holding her in his arms. She felt safe and loved. He gently touched her little forehead and said, "My child, I told you I will get you flowers. Be careful about where you walk and whom you are with. I will take care of you. You should always hold my hand as you walk along. Don't let go of my hand."

They sat on the green grass and felt the breeze. The beautiful mountains were reflected on the streams of clear water.

The girl smiled in gratitude. "Snakes were attacking me. They bit me."

Jesus replied, "I know. Those are not just snakes. They are evil spirits who try to hurt you and other people."

"What are evil spirits?" she asked in surprise.

"My child, there's a spiritual world that you cannot see with your own eyes. You can feel it though. When you felt their attack, they really were attacking you. There are spiritual realms that you need to know about. In your journey, you will encounter evil spirits many times. You can overcome those forces only in my name. You will be able to learn how to fight if you always walk with me."

"I will stay with you. I don't want the snakes to bite me again. You are the only one who seems to care for me and you are the only one who seems to know how to help me. For a long time, I didn't think I had any reason to live. You gave me hope to live. Would you tell me about your nail marks again? I still don't understand why you had to suffer for me."

Jesus looked at his nail marks then into her eyes and said, "These are marks that show I suffered for you. I died for you so you can be forgiven, have eternal life, and live with me in my Father's house forever."

Jesus' words had power, more power than anything in the world. She saw her true self for the first time. She felt ashamed of her filthy rags. Then she realized that what Jesus said was true. She was a sinner and needed God's forgiveness. Understanding why Jesus died for her sins, she felt remorse and asked God for forgiveness.

21

"My loving daughter, I died for you; you are forgiven. Now I am alive!"

Then a drop of blood fell from Jesus' nail mark and touched the girl's dress. At once, her ragged clothes changed to a beautiful, glowing dress, seamless, and whiter than snow. Her eyes opened wide. She understood how much Jesus loved her. No one else would die for her sins. Jesus was the one who not only cleaned her dress and made her feel clean, but also cleaned her soul. She felt free, as though all of her problems disappeared. She didn't have any more pain, but instead had joy and peace in her heart. She thanked Jesus again and again for his redemptive work on the cross.

"Remember your clothes were dirty, but I cleaned them. I washed your sins with my tears and my blood, which I shed on the cross. Now I am alive forever, and I am going to help you to get to our Father's home safely," Jesus said gently.

"What about my sister? She walked in the thorn bushes many times and got hurt. How I wished I could give her flowers to make her happy, but I didn't have any to give her. I saw tears in her big eyes many times when our mother got hurt. I wanted to see her smiling face someday, but now she is dead, and there is no way I can help her."

"My loving daughter, she is not dead but alive. She is also one of my children and is already safely in our eternal home. She is waiting for you, praying for your safe journey."

The girl was comforted, knowing she had something to look forward to.

5. A Thorn in the Rose

They started walking again. The road was getting worse. As she was passing through a village, some kids on the road gave her a beautiful rose. She was so happy to have a flower, but as soon as she held the rose in her hands, the thorns poked her and made her bleed.

Jesus looked at her sadly, "My child, throw away that rose. It has thorns. It makes your hand bleed."

"Jesus, it's the only flower I have. I would like to keep it."

"My child, I will provide you with many flowers with no thorns."

"Where would those be?" the girl asked impatiently.

"When we get to a flower garden, you can pick what you want," Jesus smiled.

"I want to keep this one until I get to the flower garden," she insisted.

"Child, you hurt and bleed when you hold on to it."

"I don't understand why my hands bleed. I am not holding it too tight."

"It's because if you hold on to some things, they will only

hurt you and make your life worse. Forgiving and forgetting is better than holding on."

The girl then understood. She was holding onto resentments and had an unforgiving heart toward those who hurt her. She reluctantly let go of the flower and felt a big, heavy burden lifted off of her back. She felt freer than ever. As she started walking with Jesus, she asked, "Lord, why is this journey so long and painful?"

"My loving child, that's what life is about. Look at my hands. I have suffered for you, so you don't have to suffer after this life. You will suffer in this life whenever you go through the valley of the shadow of death. Many people go through the deep, dark valley, and I want you to remember I am always with you. You may not even feel that I am with you when you are sleeping with tears and sorrow. Remember, those are the times that I cry because you are hurting. Hold on to me. I will help you to see that my grace is sufficient in all circumstances. I will wipe away your tears and give you peace and joy. Just keep walking with me."

"Jesus, what does suffering do?"

"The times you suffer are the jewels of your crown when you arrive in your eternal home. You will be rewarded when you get to our eternal home."

"I would like to get to our home fast," the girl said eagerly.

"You have many roads that you have to travel to get to the eternal home, some good and some bad. Keep hanging on to me; then you will be able to handle the situations. You could even be able to help other hurting people along the road."

"Lord Jesus, I didn't know others were hurting. I thought I was the only one who had problems."

"Yes, there are many who need help. I died to save them, and they need to hear the message. Whoever believes in me will be forgiven and receive eternal life. People who don't believe in me will suffer in this life and will also suffer terribly in their next life. That's why I came and died, so they could believe and be saved."

Now she understood what Jesus was saying. The girl knew it was Jesus who had helped her in her toughest times, and there was no question that Jesus died for her to save her from eternal suffering.

6. People in the Desert

They came to the desert and the sun was high. It was extremely hot, but somehow she was not bothered by it. Jesus was with her, and he told her many things about himself. She was delighted to learn about him. She knew Jesus meant a lot to her. Occasionally, he gave her food and water. He found shelter for her when it got too hot. She felt loved. Walking with Jesus was much easier than walking by herself.

Then, Jesus talked about how others walking through the desert were not getting any help because they didn't know him. "My child, if you want to help other hungry and thirsty people on the road, I will give you bread and water so that you can share with others."

Jesus then showed her how much some people were suffering from attacks of evil spirits. These too she could help with Jesus' power. "You can help them with prayers. I will help you overcome all these."

The girl quickly asked, "What about my flowers?"

"If you decide to help these people, it will take longer to get the flowers. I assure you that if you don't get the flowers in this life because you decide to help others, you will receive a hundred times more flowers when you reach my kingdom."

She thought for a moment, then she said, "I want to have flowers as soon as possible. I know if I don't have them soon, others will tease me again. I don't want to get hurt any more."

Jesus seemed to understand how she felt.

7. Garden City

It was a long, rough journey. Jesus taught her more about himself as he took her to a town called Wonderful Garden City. Jesus answered her prayers. When she saw the beautiful garden she was overjoyed. She picked many flowers and Jesus brought her as many as she could hold. She was dancing as she left the flower garden. If she had known she would get all the flowers she wanted, she probably wouldn't have cried bitterly when others teased her. She didn't know then that Jesus would keep his word. She thanked Jesus again and again. She knew there would be no one else like Jesus. Jesus made a crown with some flowers and put it on her head, which made her feel like a princess. Jesus gave her what her parents had denied her.

Jesus also gave her bread and juice, and she enjoyed it immensely. Jesus took care of her as he taught her about himself. She became a young woman, about to get married. Somehow she was always a little girl to Jesus, and she didn't quite understand it. As her body and soul were fed, she was satisfied. She felt loved because her husband loved and cared for her more than anyone else she had met on the road, there would be no one else like Jesus. Jesus was the only one who could satisfy her soul.

Her husband, who loved Jesus, was obedient to him when Jesus told him about the importance of helping hurting people on the road. Even though Jesus was important to her, she felt resentful when Jesus convinced her husband to feed the hungry. When she tried to change her husband's mind, Jesus told her that her husband was going to fight the good fight, and she should support her husband. Even though it was difficult, she tried to listen to Jesus. Still, she struggled because she didn't care about others who were starving on the road. It would have been easier if she hadn't been there to see her husband helping them.

8. Building a House

She was thankful her husband was a wonderful father. Their two children were gifts from God. It was delightful to watch how her husband provided love and security for his family. Her wounds were healed as she watched how her husband loved and cared for their children. Her own father hadn't been able to give her love and security, but her husband was able to give both to their children. She knew it was because of Jesus that she received many blessings in life, so she thanked Jesus many times.

Her family life was stable, and she didn't think she needed anything else. Slowly, she began to forget about the terrible roads she had traveled and about how Jesus had helped her. Everything seemed to be going well as her family had a picnic every day on the road.

When they approached a town, she saw many nice houses. Up to that point, she hadn't had any desire to have a house or build one. Now her interests had changed. She was heading toward the eternal home with Jesus, but she was getting tired on the long journey. People seemed to enjoy settling down and having homes, so she thought she had every right to enjoy life on earth, just like others.

She wanted her husband to help her build a home. She tried to change her husband's mind about following Jesus' plan, but she couldn't. Even though her husband was doing a good thing, sometimes she was impatient that he was busy feeding others instead of helping her. She even told her husband that he should work for something he could see, not for the things he couldn't see. The physical world was more important to her than the spiritual world. Her husband didn't agree with her, though. Before she got married, she had asked Jesus for a man who loved Jesus, but now she realized her husband loved Jesus more than she wanted.

Again, without even asking Jesus what he thought about her plan, she let go of his hand. She was determined to build a home without Jesus. As the beams went up and the house began to have a structure, she was thrilled at the thought of living in her own home. She didn't even miss Jesus.

She built a beautiful house, which she loved. Then she started building more houses to sell to secure her future. One day, a tornado came and destroyed everything. She was shocked. Thinking she should make the building more secure, she learned how to build a house from professionals and started again. This time an unexpected flood went through town and destroyed her house. Everything was covered with mud; she felt hopeless. She didn't have flood insurance to cover the loss.

Others didn't seem to have any problems building a nice

house. Why was she having such a disastrous time? She had to pay the workers but didn't have enough money. She cried through many sleepless nights. Then she remembered Jesus. She had not had any problems like that when she was walking with him. The problems started when she started building her permanent home in a town. She cried, "Jesus, where are you?" Jesus didn't answer, not like other times. She felt she was far away from him. She was desperate. She cried again, "Jesus, come and save me. I need your help. Where are you?" Again, to her disappointment, Jesus didn't come to her.

This time she wondered if Jesus was real. Doubts arose as she desperately looked for Jesus. "Jesus, if you are real, show yourself to me. Why don't you answer me?" she cried. She knew Jesus was real because she had walked with him before. Then a thought came to her mind: if she were to go back and find out where she had lost him, she might be able to find him.

9. Searching for Jesus

As she was going back to the roads she had come from, she asked different people on the road if they had seen Jesus, but they couldn't help her. Finally, she came to a familiar road. She saw Jesus and he was delighted to see her.

"I am sorry, Jesus. I didn't know how I lost you, but now I do. I left you here alone. Now I know you didn't leave me, but I left you! I shouldn't have just relied on my memory of the Scriptures. I thought I knew enough, but I didn't. Now I know I should walk with you and learn about you moment by moment." Jesus had to be the most important person in her life. He was the only one who could satisfy her.

"My loving child, I have been waiting for you to come back to me. I was praying all the time that you would find a way back to me," Jesus said, "Here, I will wash your feet."

She felt Jesus' familiar, gentle hands. Somehow, Jesus

seemed to find water whenever he wanted. After he washed her feet, he wiped her tears dry and embraced her tightly. Her body and soul felt clean, and she felt loved.

Jesus looked at her eyes with a smile. "My loving daughter, remember that we are on a journey to our eternal home, but before we reach there, we have some work to do as we go along."

"What kind of work?" she asked.

"You remember I told you that there are many people who are hungry and thirsty? Many people need to hear that I have died for their sins so they can believe in me and will be able to live in my Father's house with me eternally."

"Lord, my husband is already working for you. Don't you think one out of four is good enough? My two kids are too little and I have to build a house since my husband doesn't have time to help me."

"If you do my work, I will take care of you."

"Can you wait for a while, so I can finish the house that I started building?"

"My child, if you spend all your time building a house in this temporary world, you won't have any time to do more important things, like building your home in heaven. When you work for me and are fruitful, you will be building your house in an eternal home. What's more important? There are many who need to understand my love and to be saved. There is plenty of work but the workers are few. You sometimes wonder why there is not much good happening in this country. You asked me many times why you don't see miracles in the United States. You asked me why church people's spirituality seems so shallow. That's because people are not willing to work for me, just like you. Many of my children are only interested in their own comfort and don't seek the kingdom of God first."

She thought for a moment. Even though she realized that Jesus had taken care of her when she needed help, she now realized that she didn't have much trust in Jesus. She found delight in things that she could see more than the things she couldn't see. She was more interested in material wealth and she was delighted whenever she could see the improvements on her building.

10. Wounded People

Knowing that she was not ready to do his work, Jesus suggested that she spend ten percent of her time in prayer every day.

In her prayer time, Jesus taught her about the Holy Spirit, who could help her to do Jesus' work. There was no way she could have remained on her prayer journey if the Holy Spirit hadn't awakened her in the morning with hymns and kept reminding her to go back to pray when she was tired of going to church.

Jesus took her by the hand and led her to a remote field where many wounded people were lying, crying out in pain. There were nurses and doctors, but there were many wounded people who were not receiving any care.

She was horrified. "You can heal those people as you have healed me. I know you can," she pleaded.

"I have given my power to my workers. The harvest field is ready but workers are few. I need more workers to heal and help these people. This is not a permanent place for you. You don't realize that the house you are building has a shaky foundation. It will crumble when you think everything is fine. There will be others who need help along the road. I want to hire you to do my work and I will take care of you."

"Jesus, I cannot do this kind of work. You asked me to pray for them. I will pray for them. I will pray to God so he can send more workers."

32

"My loving Child, you are expecting your brothers and sisters to fight in the front against evil forces. Think about how many are battling in the war zone. These wounded people are just the few you can see. You need to go out to the front to fight the spiritual battle. When you try to avoid your responsibility, you cannot grow spiritually. When you don't fight the battle, there is more of a chance you could be working for the enemy, because it is easy to be deceived by the devil. You have to put on the full armor of God and fight the good fight. People who put on the full armor of God and fight with my mighty power are the only ones who can win the battle and help other wounded saints. Otherwise, you will end up getting hurt, like what happened before. You have to learn how to defend yourself when enemies attack you. Many of my children don't know about this battle and get hurt. They don't know how to fight and help others. The more you help wounded people, the stronger you will grow. I will give you more strength when you are fighting against strong enemies. I know you cannot do it with your own power, but when you work for me I will give you power to do it."

"What is that power?" she asked.

"My power is my word. My word is medicine for the wounded people. You are not going out there alone. I am sending you with the Holy Spirit who lives in you. He is the one who will actually change people's hearts and save them. The Spirit frees people from sin and Satan. You have to spread the word so the Spirit can heal people."

She had heard about the Holy Spirit, but until now she didn't quite understand how the Spirit helped people to do God's work. "Oh, I didn't know that. I thought when I worked for you I had to use my own wisdom and my own strength to do it."

"Nothing you do for my kingdom is done by your power. What I need from you is a willing heart to help wounded people. I have done my work by dying for them so they can be forgiven. All you have to do is be my messenger and tell others what I have done for them. If you walk close to me and learn from me, then I will teach you how to help others."

"Lord Jesus, I understand now why you are calling me again and again to do your work. Is it possible that I could make lots of money and help others who work for you?"

"I am the one who provides for all my workers. You don't have to worry about that. I want you to follow me. Now you have to make a choice. You cannot have anything between you and me. You have to choose either money or me. You cannot love both. If you love me, you will feed my sheep."

She knew there was no way she could choose money. Jesus was the most important and powerful person in the whole world. She said, "Jesus, I am sorry. I was very selfish. I was only thinking about myself all those years. I choose you and I am going to work for you. You died for me so my life is yours."

"Now you understand. Remember you will receive rewards in God's heavenly home when you are faithful."

She asked, "What should I do to help others?"

"First, you have to get yourself ready by going through training. You need to put on the full armor of God, and you have to depend on God's mighty power to do the work. The Holy Spirit will lead you and teach you what you have to do, step by step. Just follow the instructions. You will be trained every day because you are working for me. First, you need to spend at least five hours every day with me so you can learn about me. Read the gospels over and over in order to understand what I have done to save you. You have to listen to me and talk to me in prayer every day. I like to hear your sweet voice. Nothing pleases me more than when my children recognize me by coming to my presence. If my words live in you, I will do whatever you ask. I will show you what you can do when you depend on me."

"Jesus, are you going somewhere? Are you going to be with me while I am working here?"

"I am not going anywhere. I will be with you always. You have to stay close to me all the time to keep from wandering around and getting hurt. Whenever you need me, I will be right beside you. Whenever you need help, just ask me to help you. Remember, you will have to keep walking with me and talking to me through prayer. Keep studying my words. They will help you learn about me and you will know how to overcome the evil one. My word is like the sword which can help you win the battle. If you don't walk with me, my power cannot work through you. Remember, you have to love me with all your heart, mind, soul, and strength. Don't let anything come between you and me, not even yourself. You cannot follow me if you love yourself more than me. I love you so much, and I want you to love me."

11. A Dirty Dress

She was walking with Jesus for a while, then felt a heavy burden in her heart. She remembered how her dress had been dirty and spotted with blood in the old days. "Lord, I don't think I can help these people," she cried. "I know I am a sinner. You know I have made many mistakes."

Jesus gently touched her forehead. "My child, all your sins are forgiven. When I died on the cross, all your sins were nailed to the cross and died too. When I rose from the dead, your spirit also rose, blameless, clothed with my righteousness and holiness. I don't remember your sins anymore. I forgave you for my own sake because I love you. That's why I sacrificed myself for you."

She cried again, "I don't feel like I am forgiven."

Jesus spread his hands, and drops of blood from the nail wounds fell to her dress. Her dress shone brighter and brighter, and she felt clean. Deep in her heart, she understood she was forgiven. All her burdens were lifted from her. She knew then what Jesus had said was right. The words of God had the power to make her spirit, soul, and body clean. "Thank you Jesus, for dying for my sins. Your words have so much power," she exclaimed with joy.

"Now, you know why I am asking you to go out and tell others about me. Many carry big burdens like you used to. My words have power to set them free from their sins and from the devil. The devil has been lying to people, accusing them, and has many people in chains. Nothing but my words and the Holy Spirit can save them from the devil. Go and tell others that they don't have to carry their burdens anymore. Tell them I died for their sins and they are forgiven."

As they walked together, she started weeping, "I just don't think I can do it. I think others might tease me if I say I want to try to help other wounded people. I feel so inadequate. I am only a child. I live in a foreign land. Now I have forgotten

my native tongue, and I am not good with my second language. Jesus, there are many others who could speak for you better than me. Are you sure you picked the right person to do your work? How can I teach others? I am only a child."

He said, "I want you to read the story of Moses until you are convinced that I will teach you what to say and give you the words to speak."

She read the story of Moses over and over and was convinced Jesus would help her. It wouldn't be her power, but Jesus' power. "Yes, Jesus, you rescued me many times. You are the most loving and powerful person I know. You saved me from my sins and from Satan. Now I believe you can help me to do your work. My life is yours. Use me for your kingdom as you want."

12. A Feast

She felt so small as she walked down the road, because she saw so many wounded people. She cried, "Jesus, I feel too inadequate to work for you. I don't think I am good enough to do your work."

"My child, that's exactly why I'm calling you to do my work. If you feel adequate then you won't depend on me or my power, but on yourself. I can only use people who will depend on me instead of their own wisdom, knowledge or abilities. I can even use a donkey to speak. You should rely on me. I will teach you what to speak because I will be with you always. When you feel like you could do it yourself, when you think you could help me with your own abilities, then realize that you are failing, because you cannot do anything unless my power works through you. My power won't work in people who depend on themselves to do my work. In every step and every situation, depend on me. Then I will show you wonders, and I will go out and touch people's hearts. Just love me and walk close to me. Let's go and help others. Many people are suffering. Help them so they can help others. I called many of my children to work, but they didn't believe my power. Because of their feelings of inadequacy, many have turned away from me. I don't want you to do that. Follow me."

She followed him. It was a sweet communion. Spending time with Jesus gave her such delight; she wondered why she hadn't followed Jesus before. Jesus took her to a huge church where many of Jesus' workers were having a feast. Many sat before Jesus and shared the meal with him. While they were eating, they received instructions from the Holy Spirit on how to help others. When they left, some carried big and others carried small loaves of bread and buckets of water to feed the hungry and thirsty.

"My Lord Jesus, why do some carry out lots of food and others carry just a little?"

"My loving child, that's what I wanted to show you. My father has a big bakery in the universe and a bottomless living well. People who carry out lots of bread and water are the ones who listen to my teaching and the Holy Spirit's instruction, and they know how many people they have to feed. They also listen to my words and obey. They live godly lives, and they have more time to feed more people. Those who carry out a small amount of food are the ones who don't spend much time with me. They are too busy listening to the world and themselves. They don't have time to talk to me, so they don't give me any time to talk to them. Consequently, they don't have much time to listen to the Holy Spirit's instruction, and they don't know whom to feed. Not only do they not have time to eat at my table, but they take out only little amounts of food. Their sheep are hungry and thirsty, just like their leader. Follow me, I have something else to show you."

Jesus took her to the outside of the church, and she saw many little bakeries built by different people. Jesus said, "I have called these people to work, but they have their own ideas of how to feed people. Instead of relying on my power and spending time with me, these people started their own bakeries and dug their own wells. What they don't realize is that my bread and water is the only food that can nourish people and make them grow spiritually. They don't rely on me. They don't pay attention to my words, and they don't listen to me in prayer. How I wish they would talk to me! They listen to the world more than to me. When they are occupied with things other than me, I cannot talk to them. They spend lots of time agonizing about baking bread and trying to draw water from the dry ground, and their flocks are starving. What I want most from my disciples is for them to walk closely with me. I want their love more than their devotion to their work. They can bear much fruit if they listen and learn from me. They cannot bear much fruit when they don't walk with me. Many of my workers are hungry and dying because they don't come to my feast. They don't realize that they can only feed others after they have fed their souls by eating at my table. I want you to know this, so you will remember to walk with me; this way you can be fruitful."

She was glad to hear that Jesus wanted her to walk with him always. She knew how much she was enjoying walking with him. She started singing about how much she loved him and Jesus looked more pleased than ever. She had everything she needed. She had Jesus.

Jesus said to her, "You are my witness. Come and eat at my table."

13. A Precious Stone

She took one of her precious stones out of her pocket as she followed Jesus. They had been given to her as gifts from God a while ago, and she played with them and was delighted to look at them whenever she could. Some stones looked polished and bright, as if they were little lights, but the one she took out was scratched and looked cloudy and dim. She was alarmed and tried to rub it to make it shine like it had before, but she couldn't. She started weeping.

"Jesus, can you fix this? I don't know what happened, but one of my children seems to have forgotten about you. How can this be? I am trying so hard, but it doesn't seem to help. Please help me and my child."

Jesus stretched out his hands and said, "Why don't you give your child to me so I can help her."

She hesitated. The stone had her child's name on it, and was too precious for her to give to anyone, even to Jesus. She tried to rub it again to make it shine, but she couldn't. "I don't understand what happened to my child. I would give even my life to make this shine again," she cried and cried. She felt hopeless. She sat on the ground and wept as Jesus looked sadly at her. She didn't want to get up and tried to shine the stone with her handkerchief. It didn't work. She seemed to forget that she was supposed to follow Jesus.

Jesus asked her, "Am I not greater than your problems?"

She thought about it for a while. Jesus was right. He was greater and more powerful than anyone else she had met. "Yes, you are greater than my problems." She wiped her tears.

"My child, why don't you give me all the stones? When you go out to a spiritual battlefield, you cannot work effectively if you carry all the stones you have in your pocket. It will slow you down, and you won't be concentrating on what I want you to do."

"Lord, I gave my life to you, so you could use me the way

41

you want. Don't you think that's good enough?"

"I want you to give me everything you have. You have to hand it all over to me so I can help you be a better worker for my kingdom."

She got up and took the remaining precious stones from her pocket. Some were prettier than others, and some were just plain rocks. Each one had on it the names of her family, her relatives, her finances, her future, her ministry work for Jesus, and many others. She had even forgotten the names of some stones because she had picked them up on the road a long time ago. She gathered all of them and gave them to Jesus. He then put all of them in his pocket and said, "I am going to ask my Father to take care of all these stones for you. I will ask him to shine them and keep them safe while you are on the battlefield."

She felt free. She had given all of her problems to Jesus. She was comforted that Jesus would take care of them. As she walked along, she collected more stones out of habit and put them in her pocket.

Jesus told her, "Give them to me. I will take care of them. The problems in your life are tests of your faith. You will pass the tests when you give everything to me. I have taken your burdens, and I have overcome the world. You need to take care of others who need help, and you can do that only if you keep giving me the stones that you collect on the way. Come, follow me. You are my disciple if you do what I ask you to do."

She gave all of the stones to Jesus. She sang hymns of how much Jesus had done for her as she followed him. Her heart was filled with joy when she saw Jesus' smiling face.

14. Mountain of Testing

They soon approached a gravel road. She couldn't understand why the nice road suddenly turned rocky. The gravel road disappeared and before them were tall, steep mountains covered with rocks and sagebrush.

They started climbing mountains. They had to slow down more now than ever because there were so many rocks. She wondered if her journey would ever end. It certainly would be easier if Jesus would move the mountain and make the road straight. She knew Jesus could do that. Jesus had also told her earlier that if she had faith, even she could move the mountains. Where was her faith? She couldn't understand. She expected that everyone would rejoice when she decided to follow Jesus instead of following the world. She was wrong. Her husband, who was also Jesus' disciple, was not happy. He said that when she followed Jesus, she might end up working away from him. He was not against her decision, but she knew how reluctant he was to support it. How could she make him understand that following Jesus was more important than following his ideas?

Jesus knew her thoughts. He told her, "This mountain is called a mountain of testing. Climbing this mountain path is more dangerous and difficult than any other path. I called many people by giving them the desire to serve me and to be my full-time disciples. Many responded, but when they arrived here and saw this big mountain they gave up, because they thought they had to move the mountain with their own power. They paid more attention to their environment, listened to their families, listened to other people, and listened to themselves, but they didn't listen to me. Some decided to become part-time workers for their own convenience, therefore they were not able to do much work. Many wandered around on this mountain for a long time because they were not willing to give up their love for money and worldly desires. In later life, a few realized how they had abandoned their calling and then followed me. You will face many fires of testing on this mountain to see if you can be my disciple. These are purifying fires to help you be a better disciple. Some turned away from me and abandoned me when they saw the fires. They didn't realize the fires would only make them strong and mighty in God's sight. Unless you explore and learn about this mountain as you walk with me, you won't be able to move any mountains along the way. Remember, it is I who called you to do my work. Don't let anyone or any circumstances change your mind or stop you from following me. Pay attention to the Spirit's instructions and obey him. Otherwise, you will end up wandering around on this mountain and will grieve me greatly. One of your jobs is to recognize those wandering workers of mine and encourage them to stay on course."

"You are going to teach me how to move the mountains?"

"Yes, my child. It is I who will help you do that. Pray for your husband and forgive him. I will be helping you to do my work, he will not. I already told you from the beginning that I am the one who will provide all the training and education you need to do my work. The Holy Spirit is your professor and your guide. You shouldn't build resentment against your husband. He is going through fires of testing which will purify him to make him a better disciple. To give is to receive. When you forgive, I will answer your prayers. When you pray for him, I will bless him and I will bless you. Test me, and see if I answer your prayers. From now on, I will teach you what is ahead on the road as long as you walk with me. Then, through my power, you will be prepared to move the mountains along the way."

15. An Artist

Not long after that, she found a box of colored crayons on the road. She picked it up and on the flat surface of a rock nearby began drawing a mountain and trees. A group of travelers passing by stopped and looked at her drawing. "You must be an artist," one man said.

She was pleased with the comment and kept drawing. She thought she must be special and deserved recognition. She was an average art student, but she thought that if she practiced more, she could be an artist. She was so involved in drawing that she forgot about Jesus, who was standing there waiting.

Jesus leaned against the edge of the rock and asked, "Do you remember what I have been warning you about these last two weeks?" The sun was bright, and the gentle breeze moved Jesus' soft hair; his face was filled with compassion.

She stopped drawing a house and paused to think what Jesus was talking about. Then she remembered what had happened. As she had spent time with the Lord, she had learned how to take God's bread and water to those in need. When people started thanking her and showing her appreciation, she became proud. She knew the bread and water were from Jesus, that she was just a carrier. She should have told people to give glory to God; instead, she entertained the thought that she was better than other people.

"Yes, Lord, you have been warning me through Peter's and James' letters. I didn't understand why the Holy Spirit kept asking me to read those passages again and again, but now I know. God resists the proud but gives grace to the humble. I didn't realize how others' recognition could bring out my proud attitude. I am very sorry. I don't know how you can put up with me. Please forgive me. I learned earlier that I didn't have a forgiving heart, and now I am learning that I don't have a humble heart."

"Remember this. If you look for praise or recognition from other people while feeding my sheep, you will be working for yourself, not for me or my kingdom. In fact, some of my workers love their work more than me. They love praise from people and forget about praise from my Father," Jesus told her. "I have abandoned many of my workers because they served themselves instead of serving me. Some of them don't realize the power of the Holy Spirit and rely on themselves, so they are not effective in their ministry. Some experience the power of the Holy Spirit, become proud, and give themselves the glory which belongs to me. The Holy Spirit abandons their ministry and they cannot be effective anymore. I give the Holy Spirit to my children so the Spirit can teach them and they can be my witness, not to feed their self-glorification or pride. I give power to my workers to go out and tell others about me so they can release the Holy Spirit's saving power to free people from sin and Satan."

"You helped me to forgive others by helping me to understand other people and situations. Please help me to have a humble heart," she said, tears rolling down her cheeks.

46

"Most of the time, when someone is praised and honored by other people, they are not the one God will praise and honor. Show respect to everyone because you don't know whom God will honor and praise. Also, when you praise people in front of others, it will create jealousy, resentment, and discouragement among my workers. The devil uses that to create division among my people. That's why I said anyone who wants to be the first must be the servant of all. So be careful what you do to others and to yourself. If you remember to give God glory for all the work you do for my kingdom, then the Holy Spirit will work with you, and you will bear lots of fruit."

"Jesus, I am learning that if I could see myself the way you see me, then there would be no room for boasting or a proud attitude," she said, looking up into Jesus' gentle eyes.

"There is one thing of which you can be proud," Jesus explained. "You can be proud of me because of what I have done for you. Anything else that makes you proud or boastful will lead you to fall. You cannot even boast about your accomplishment because you wouldn't be able to accomplish anything without the help of the Spirit. As you know, the Spirit is the one who opens people's hearts and saves them. You know that you cannot do anything productive for my kingdom without me. Your obedience will be rewarded in my Father's heavenly home. Your reward on earth is to walk with me, guided by the Holy Spirit, so you can see my mighty power going out to save people. If you receive all the glory and recognition from the people on earth, you don't get any reward when you reach my Father's house. The Holy Spirit's power will work through you when you are willing to obey the Spirit's leading and to do what I asked of you with a humble heart."

16. Feed Them

Soon after this conversation with her, a friend came and asked the girl to bring more bread and water for the hungry.

The girl hesitated. She then remembered what Jesus had told her before. He told her to rely on him at every step and in every situation, so she asked, "Jesus, I don't know if I should feed other people anymore. Wouldn't it be better if I just ignore this request to save myself from falling into the sin of pride? Do I need to tell others what I learned from you?"

"Yes, you need to feed the hungry. That's why I have called you. Tell them what you have learned, that will feed the hungry souls. If you don't tell them, I will raise others up to tell them. There are many people who need to hear what you have learned from me. Some of my children have forgotten me. You need to remind them that I am the one who feeds the hungry souls through my workers. They need to hear that I am alive and that I care about them."

"Lord Jesus, my sins of pride and a boastful heart are not my only problems. I am also afraid of other people's criticism. There are some people, even Christians, who don't understand me. They mock me when I share about my walk with you and what I am learning from you."

"My daughter, don't be afraid of others' rejection or criticism. I am always with you. Just tell them that I asked you to share what you have learned from me. You have to listen to me, not to people. You have been asking me why you don't see a big revival in America. There have been revivals in some parts of America, but my desire is to have more of them. I am looking for a tool that can be used by the Holy Spirit to touch many people's hearts, so that they turn their hearts to me and my Father. That tool is someone who will listen to me, not to other people. I want you to keep praying for revival. Your prayers will be answered when I find enough people to give all their hearts, all their minds, all their souls, and all their strength to me for my kingdom and for revival in this country. You can be a part of that revival if you are willing to give all of yourself and to pay attention to the Holy Spirit's leading. Rely on my wisdom, not on yours."

That made sense to the girl. She realized she was not indispensable. Jesus could raise anyone to accomplish what he wanted to be done. Jesus loved her and was not going to force her to do anything she was not willing to do. She didn't have to be afraid of people because Jesus was with her. She had a choice of being obedient or disobedient. She chose to be obedient. "Thank you, Jesus. You have answered my questions. I will feed these people."

"Come and follow me. I will show you how much work we have to do before the biggest revival begins. I want you to reach out in places not many people reach out to, because that's where my lost sheep are," Jesus held her hands tightly. "My child, I love you. I will be with you and take care of you."

The girl was delighted to hear what Jesus had said. Her heart was filled with admiration for Jesus, and she said, "You are the most important person in my life. No one else in the world loves me as you do. You died for my sins, so that I could be forgiven. You are walking with me, so that you can lead my way to the heavenly home. You are helping me to help others, so they can also find the way to your glorious heavenly home. Jesus, you are the best. Thank you for being with me. I have everything I need because I have you."

She started skipping and dancing while squeezing Jesus' hands. Jesus' face glowed as he started skipping and dancing with her. She looked into Jesus' eyes and started to sing to him, "I praise you and love you, Jesus, with all my heart. I love you more than yesterday. You have power over everything. If you ask me what I want, I want revival in this country. Holy Spirit, open people's hearts so they can understand they are sinners, repent, and be saved. Jesus, I give you glory, praise, honor, and thanks, because you deserve it. I love you more today than yesterday."

She knew walking with Jesus was difficult sometimes, but she also realized walking with Jesus was the most wonderful and glorious walk she could have.

Reflection

I used to say that if everyone were like me, there would be no pastors. Jesus changed my heart. Still, I had many questions before I began attending the Iliff School of Theology.

One question was whether God wanted me to attend school at this time. In order to attend Iliff, which is located in Denver, Colorado, I had to drive six or seven hours on Monday to attend classes, stay through Thursday and drive back home that night. Our daughter was fifteen and our son was twelve. Would my husband be able to handle work and the kids? Would it be better if I waited until our children got older?

While struggling with these questions, different images came to my mind. I believe God gave them to me because those images had spiritual lessons for me. I finished writing *Journey With Jesus*, but I didn't do anything about it for a while. When those images kept coming to my mind, I thought God was telling me that I was not done with the story; I started writing Part Two.

To my amazement, Jesus answered the questions I had concerning school while I was writing the story. Thus, I was able to go to school with peace of mind, believing that God was directing me there.

Like Part One of *Journey With Jesus*, I felt blessed while I was writing Part Two. As I was writing, I became aware that most of my stories evaluated my life and mostly my failures. Why? If Christ was leading me and I had more commitment to follow Jesus' calling, should I not see a more successful and comforting journey? Strangely, the answer was no.

Some of my friends who read my stories told me that

Part Two helped their spiritual journey more than the first because it explained what they should watch out for as Christians. One friend told me that the first one was positive but the second one was negative, and I agreed with her. She was my good friend, and I valued her opinion so highly that I decided to discard the story.

However, before I put the story away, I reviewed the lessons I learned. That so changed my mind that I decided to keep it. Part Two gave me a new perspective of myself, other Christians, and Jesus. The most important lesson I learned was this: Jesus is willing to work with anyone, even a failure.

Before I started writing Part Two, I thought I had lived a pretty good life; therefore, I considered myself a pretty good Christian, according to my own standard, of course. While I was writing, I realized I had failed miserably as a Christian because I was naive and ignorant about the dangers Christians have to go through.

I understood the spiritual world from my early Christian experience, and I should have paid more attention to my spiritual walk, but I only paid attention to the physical world. I accepted Christ and experienced his love and forgiveness, but I didn't realize that I had to have a total commitment to follow Jesus. Consequently, when I felt God calling me to full-time ministry, I resisted. I wanted to follow my desires and those of the world.

The price of not walking with Jesus was high. I paid a great price for my weaknesses with regret and remorse. I learned that it is good to be reminded of our mistakes, but not to beat ourselves up with the sins that we had repented and been forgiven for. Instead, we just need to remind ourselves not to make the same mistakes. In that sense, it was good that Jesus helped me to evaluate my life.

I think that from the beginning, I was aware that the story of Part Two was an answer to my prayer. Previously, I had asked God to help me to see myself the way He sees me.

I learned that God sees me differently than I see myself. I was humbled when I realized that I didn't even recognize my own mistakes until Jesus helped me to see them through the story. Jesus knew all my faults, but he always willingly helped me. He was so kind and gentle when I didn't even deserve it. It was painful to go back and be reminded of my mistakes, but I learned that it was necessary for my spiritual growth.

I learned that the reason Jesus was calling me to do his work was not because I lived up to His expectations, but because His grace is greater than my shortcomings. Jesus accepts and forgives people who fail him, and he even calls them to serve him. I learned that unless Jesus reveals our sins, we may not even realize how much we grieve God. That helps me to have more compassion for other Christians who make mistakes and don't even realize what they are doing.

I give God all the glory for what he has done in my life. Without Jesus' love and power, I know I would not have the peace of mind that I have now. Without Jesus' encouragement and assurance, I know I wouldn't have the courage to follow him. Without Jesus' compassion, I know this story couldn't have been written.

I was driving to school one morning in Denver and saw a little girl, two or three years old, holding her father's hand, going into a store. The father opened and held the door so the girl could walk in. She was so little and helpless, there was no way she could comprehend her father's feelings and thoughts. Seeing that, I realized how little I could understand my heavenly Father, even when I tried so hard. The love the man showed toward the little girl was something I needed to remember. God, my loving Father, was leading my life, and He would care for me as though I were a little child. Realizing that, I broke down in tears. Even if no one cared, I knew God would care for me. I needed that assurance.

The scene of the father and the little girl stayed in my mind for many days and reminded me how much my heavenly

Father loves me. It also reminded me of my relationship with Jesus. I was a young woman, but whenever I saw myself with Jesus, I was a little girl, holding Jesus' hand.

For a long time, even after I became a Christian, I was walking by myself. I thought my ideas were better than Jesus'. I wanted to follow my own plans. I took a wrong path and wandered around the desert in despair. I was headed toward the wide road of destruction, but Jesus called me and turned me around. Since then, I learned why I fell away from the Lord, why I didn't feel the presence of God in my life, and why I had a big empty hole in my heart. It was because I was not walking with Jesus. I learned that there was no way I could ignore Jesus. He was part of me. I wouldn't be able to feel whole without Jesus, because the empty hole I had in my heart was a place prepared only for him. I knew I desperately needed Jesus to walk with me so I could listen to and talk to him.

Jesus knew how to help me better than anyone else I had met along the road. He took care of me whenever I was hungry or thirsty. Whenever I walked on the dirt road, he washed my feet, as he always had. He forgave me when I made mistakes. Jesus' blood had so much power to clean my heart. I knew there was no one else like him. He loved me so much that he had even given his life, dying on the cross, taking my place so I could be forgiven. After Jesus finally convinced me of how important it is to feed the spiritually hungry and thirsty, I told him I would serve him. I didn't realize how much he had to teach me until I made that final commitment to follow him. One thing I knew for sure: Jesus would always be with me, so my journey with Jesus continued.

Part Two:
Journey With Jesus

17. A Game Room

The girl said, "My Lord, I want you to help me see the way you see me, so I don't fall away from you again." The air was fresh and Jesus' face was bright with a gentle smile, his eyes filled with love and compassion.

Jesus said, "My beloved daughter, I will show you how I see you and tell you the dangers for people who decide to follow me. The devil knows whom I have called to ministry, and tries to encourage my workers to abandon their calling. One thing you have to learn is not to love the world, but to love me. I will show you what happens when people love the world. Come, follow me."

Jesus showed her to a game room which had in it a spinning metal rod surrounded with sharp blades. Many people had tried to hold or touch the blades, and the blade cut through their bodies. Jesus turned to the girl. "People play this game because they believe gaining money, wealth, and worldly things will lead to security. Many try to obtain worldly possessions to gain security, but the only security they can truly have is me; I am the only one who has the power to save their souls and give them eternal life. When people are satisfied with worldly possessions, they tend to forget about me and my kingdom. Do you realize why I have brought you here?"

The girl cried, "Jesus, I tried to grab a blade, and I got hurt. I relied on money, and not on you. Please forgive me."

"I forgive you, my child. In the midst of your backsliding, my grace carried you out of that room. Your financial trouble was a blessing to you. Without it, you wouldn't have started praying to me. You would have kept heading toward destruction. You were about to collapse on the floor, but I snatched you out of that room and healed you."

"I'm so sorry, Jesus. I listened to the world and myself but not to you!"

Jesus said, "When people listen to me by reading the Scriptures and praying, they leave that game room and are healed of their wounds. Once saved and healed from their wounds, they can help others get out of that place. When people end up dying in that game room, their spirits are tortured by demons forever. Many of my followers have turned back to the game rooms when they faced financial trials. They chose worldly comfort over me, bringing spiritual destruction. I cry when they don't understand why they are getting hurt, falling, and being beaten by the devil."

"Jesus, my problem was that I didn't know I was hurting myself. I had to take care of our family's financial needs. My husband didn't make enough money, and you know how much my family suffered because of it."

Jesus asked her, "While your husband was feeding the hungry, was there any time you didn't have enough food for your family?"

"No, Lord, we always had food. That was not our problem."

"My daughter, many of my workers fast when they don't have enough food to eat. I am telling you they are richer than those who have enough food. In fact, my workers fast and eat according to my wishes. They know their reward is not in this world, but rather in the heavenly home. By experiencing trials and difficulties, my workers will learn about my love and gain strength through my power. I will always be your comforter and provider. I want your total commitment to me. When you work for me and my kingdom, I will take care of you."

"Lord Jesus, the only way I made money was to work for other people. Are you asking me to work for you only? Some people work different jobs to support themselves."

Jesus said, "There are some I call to work to earn money to serve my people, but I am calling you to tell others about my love. If everyone worked only for temporal things, who would take care of the spiritually sick, the hungry, the wounded, and the dying people? I call my workers to share my love and power with others. I was training you to do my work when I sent you to school. I showed you the spiritual world to motivate you to go out to help the wounded people with my power. You experienced the power of my words. When you were backsliding and followed the wide road, money became your god. Making money was the center of your attention, not me. You didn't think about what I wanted you to do. When you worked for someone else, you had little time to do the things I wanted you to do. What did you accomplish while following the world?"

"Lord, I thought I was accomplishing a lot, but as I look back, I see I didn't accomplish anything. I didn't even realize that I was going the wrong way. Now I am worried about how we can manage our finances. My seminary education will cost so much."

Jesus answered, "Is not everything mine? Why worry so much! I will provide all the money you need for school. I train my workers and I pay for their expenses. Didn't I pay for all your school expenses before? I promise you that I will take care of you when you follow me. You will learn how to be content because my grace is sufficient for you. When you are willing to suffer and face difficulties for me and my kingdom, you will be spiritually rich in this life, and rich in my Father's kingdom."

Jesus was right. There were times she thought it was impossible for her to continue in school but Jesus opened the doors and provided everything she needed.

"Thank you, Jesus. You have helped me so far, and I am glad that you are going to help me again. Thank you for healing me from backsliding. How can I make sure that I won't deceive myself and go back to that game room again? How can I know when I love something more than you?"

"When you try to follow the Holy Spirit's directions, you, yourself, circumstances, and other people will try to hinder you. When you are filled with fear and cannot obey the Holy Spirit, that is your blocking stone. That blocking stone is what you love more than me. If you have something and are afraid of losing it, that is what you love more than me. Do not have any fears, because I will be with you. From time to time, the Holy Spirit will open others' hearts to let them know that you are walking with me. You don't have to worry about what you will lose because you don't own anything in this world. If you think you do, the devil has already fooled you. The prince of this world will try to make you believe that if you work hard, and forget about me, and worship worldly things, you will have all the riches in the world. Anything I give you in this world is for you to use in serving me and my kingdom more effectively. If you love anything more than me it will become your trap. You cannot even love your life more than me. Loving yourself more than me will cause you to pay more attention to your own desires than to my plans for you. Do you realize that your attitudes and your heart are against me? When I ask you to do something, you try to reason spiritual matters with your own wisdom, and you just cannot understand it. Thus, you disobey the Holy Spirit. That's why you have to renew your mind with my words and be instructed by the Holy Spirit. Then you will be able to do what I ask you to do. In order to bear lots of fruit, you shouldn't love the world. You have to die to the world."

"Lord, how can I die to the world when I am still alive?"

Jesus answered. "To die to the world is to die to your own fear. What matters is to do God's will."

18. Sacrifice

"Lord Jesus, when I decided to follow you, I thought I only had to give myself, but I am learning that even my family, my relatives, and my friends have to sacrifice part of their hearts and lives. That was not what I expected."

"When I call one of my children to serve me, I also call people around them to sacrifice their lives to serve me. Your commitment to serve me challenges their faith and commitment to my work. The more commitment I demand, the more sacrifices there will be, but many don't want to sacrifice themselves for me or my kingdom. Without sacrifice there is no gain. My sacrifice brought you out of the kingdom of darkness and into my kingdom of light. It broke the chains of sin and death and released you from Satan so you could walk with me. By giving your life for my kingdom, you will grow spiritually and learn to encourage others to follow me. You have received many spiritual blessings due to my sacrifice on the cross and the sacrifices of others for my kingdom. That's the sacrifice I am asking of you. You will not only have to sacrifice your life, but you should also encourage others to sacrifice their lives for me and my kingdom so my lost sheep can be found. I will take care of you and those around you. They will sacrifice their time with you to serve me while you take care of the sick, wounded, and those in need."

"Jesus, I thought my tears of offering were good enough when I decided to follow you, but I have learned that my decision to follow you will cause my loved ones to cry. They are being forced to sacrifice part of their lives for me."

"My child, you misunderstand. They are not sacrificing for you but for me and my kingdom. Their tears will become their blessing. You need to understand that without tears, there would be no healing. When you were weeping before me because you didn't want to obey the Holy Spirit's calling, your tears purified your motivation and healed you of your worldly desires. Your tears helped bring you awareness of your spiritual condition; the tears you and others shed will bring healing to many people. Whenever you cry, I cry too. Someone has planted the gospel seed, watered it with tears, and prayed for your healing. I listen and answer my children's tears of offering."

"I didn't realize others' tears can bring my healing," the girl said.

Jesus replied, "My tears and suffering brought reconciliation between people and my Father. People who sow tears will reap songs of joy. It is time to go out and sow the seeds of tears. You need to plant my seeds of love so others can understand how much I love them. You have been asking me to give you a heart for God because you want to hear what I hear, see what I see, and feel what I feel. Think about the people in the game room. How many are crying out for help? Not many have concern for these wounded, hurting, dying, and suffering people. How can you have peace in your mind when evil spirits torture my beloved people? How can you have joy in your heart when you know many are spiritually naked, wounded, and headed toward eternal torture and imprisonment? How can you sleep when my people refuse to respond to my calling because they love the world more than me? The harvest is plentiful, but the workers are few. If you have my heart, you will weep all the time. Your tears of compassion are the seeds of love that will bring healing to others. You will see miracles when you sow seeds with tears. In the midst of weeping, I give peace, joy, and strength to my people. You won't always comprehend how I feel, but sometimes I will allow you to understand, so you will know who needs you, as well as when, how, and why you should help. Now it is time to go out to look in the bushes to find my lost sheep and heal them."

"Jesus, why do I have to extend myself so much to reach out to people when I have enough work to do around my home and church as a pastor's wife?"

"Many who attend church are already healed. They need continual care, but the ones who need the most help are not in the church. Many of my lost sheep are hungry, thirsty, frightened, hurting, crying, weeping, and wailing in the desert where the scorpions and snakes roam. They need my care. I know where they are, and I see their tears of despair. Many wounded sheep are wandering around in the thorn bushes and the lonely streets where the wolves search for food. Many brokenhearted people cry for help, and I am the only one who can cure them. I need my workers to go out to heal them with my medicine of love and power and to bring them safely into my heavenly home. My medicine is free because I have already paid for it with my tears and blood. The Holy Spirit will lead you so that you can reach out to the people I want you to reach out to."

19. The Fire

The girl said, "Lord, not everyone approves of following you the way I am following you now. It was much easier for my family and my relatives before I made a commitment to serve you. Now there is more struggling."

"Do you remember I said I didn't come to bring peace but a sword, division, and fire? People who love their father or mother more than me are not worthy of me; people who love their son or daughter more than me are not worthy of me; people who don't take up their crosses and follow me are not worthy of me. Whoever finds their life will lose it, and whoever loses their life for my sake will find it. I want your total devotion for me and my kingdom. Without complete surrender to the Holy Spirit, you will wander around in the desert and try to do what you or others think you should do. Don't pay any attention to others when they try to discourage you from following me. The Holy Spirit will help you to do my work. The

Holy Spirit will go out and open people's hearts when you obey my instructions. Now you have to make a decision as to whether you will follow me or the world. You will face this question again and again until you consider yourself dead to the world but alive to me. If you look for others' approval, you will end up following the world. Did any of my disciples ask for approval from anyone when I called them to follow me? If they had, many wouldn't have followed."

"Lord, some people try to convince me that I should just help my husband in the church."

"That's because they don't understand why I have called you to the ministry."

"You understand, Lord. Why don't you tell them that you have called me to the ministry?"

"There is a reason why I don't tell them. It is for their benefit as well as yours. You don't quite understand why I called you to the ministry and how I am going to use you in the future. You have to follow me one step at a time. Through this experience you will learn to depend on me, not others. Others who don't understand you at this time will also learn to depend on me, instead of their own understanding."

"Jesus, help me to depend on you."

Jesus smiled. "Don't be afraid of anyone because I am with you. Just follow the Holy Spirit's directions. I am going to say this again: others around you will grow spiritually because of your commitment to serve me. I will show them that I am alive and that I care about them. My fire will purify you and the people around you. Follow me. I have many things to show you."

20. A Beautiful Town

Jesus led her to a beautiful town. Along the roads all types of flowers and trees were blooming. Colorful birds and wild animals could be seen along the banks of the stream that flowed through the town. People in the park were enjoying the beauty of nature. There were many houses there. Jesus stopped and knocked on the doors marked with a cross, but no one opened the doors.

Jesus said to her, "My child, many people in this town believe they are good Christians—that's why they display a cross on their doors—but they don't know me or believe that I died to save them. You need to tell them what I have done for them; they need healing."

"Jesus, I thought you wanted me to reach out to the people who are wounded and dying. Those I saw through the window don't seem to suffer from anything, so why should they listen when I tell them that they are sick and need a doctor? They will mock me if I tell them that they need you."

Jesus looked at her with a sad look in his eyes and said, "My daughter, you are only seeing what you can see. They seem to be doing fine outwardly, but deep inside they realize how empty their hearts are. They need to see themselves as I see them: naked, pitiful, and with sores all over their bodies. There are many lost sheep in this town. People who depend on themselves fall into destruction. When people focus on doing only good things and forget about me, they do not walk with me. They need to depend on me and my redemptive work on the cross, not their own work. My children are called to do good works. If doing good things doesn't help them to grow spiritually, that means they are doing good to give glory to themselves, not to give glory to me."

She realized why Jesus had taken her there. She used to try to do good things, but without seeking Jesus. She was so busy baking pies for others that she didn't realize Jesus was standing at the door, knocking, and calling her name. She knew she was missing something but she didn't know what it was. Her heart was empty because she didn't have Jesus in her heart.

"Jesus, I am sorry that I made you wait," she blurted out. "I didn't even realize that I was ignoring you. I was so busy enjoying the beauty of nature and meeting wonderful people that I totally forgot that I needed to walk with you each moment by reading the Scriptures. Thank you, Jesus, for waking me up from my horrible daydream, where I was making a thousand pies without having the right ingredients. I didn't have anything to give and I tried to give others something that didn't really matter in the end. What they needed was you, but I thought they needed me."

Jesus continued, "My words are the only tool that can unlock people's hearts. It is sad to say this, but many of my workers couldn't pass by this town. They settled here to receive people's recognition, instead of my Father's. They wanted to live in a beautiful and safe environment, not realizing that a worldly environment would numb their spiritual senses. They settled here without asking me. When people listen to the world more than me, they open their hearts to the influences of the devil. The devil told my workers that they were doing futile work if they worked for me, and they believed him. Those who quit following me are trapped in this town and don't want to follow the Holy Spirit's calling. When people make compromises with the world, they love the world more than me. My faithful workers listen to the instructions of the Holy Spirit. Then they go down to the sewer to pull out hurting people to rescue and to heal them with my words. My workers will go where I send them. I will be where my faithful workers are."

"I am learning that if I don't listen to you, I will be listening to the world. The more I listen to the world, the easier it is to fall into sin. That's how I lost my first love for you. I want you to fill my heart with your words and the Holy Spirit so that I can do what you want me to do. From now on, I will try to cut out worldly entertainment as much as possible. Help me to overcome worldly distractions with your wisdom and power.

Help me so that I can focus on you and nothing else."

"My daughter, learn from me by reading the gospels as much as you can every day. Then you will have more of me. Follow me, I have many things to show you."

21. The Black River

That night, Jesus led her to a black river where many people were crying out for help. Jesus walked on the water with her.

"My daughter, as long as you hold my hand, you are safe," he assured her.

Jesus was so powerful. His words gave her such peace of mind that she forgot she was walking on the water. In that dark place she saw lights shining from various sized ships shaped like churches. Lifeguards wore glowing garments and threw lifesavers out to pull people from the river. Some walked on the water as if it were land and listened to the Holy Spirit's instructions about how they could help people.

"I called those rescuers to serve me and they willingly went to save dying people. They are the little lights reflecting my light," Jesus said proudly. "I called them to shine their lights so that others could find the way to my Father's heavenly home."

"Jesus, why do some glow more than others?" she asked.

"Those who have brighter shining clothes are living godly lives, obeying my words and obeying the Holy Spirit's leading. The greater their commitment for me and my kingdom, the greater the light shines from them. When people have less commitment for me and for my kingdom, less light shines from their lives, and only a few come to know me and be saved."

The girl understood why she was not able to bring many people to Christ. She was not listening to the Holy Spirit's leading and didn't pay much attention to the words of Jesus to reach out to the lost souls. "I am sorry, Jesus. My lack of commitment to your calling caused me to ignore the lost people. Help me so that I will be able to reach out to people as you would want me to."

"My daughter, your obedience to the Holy Spirit's instruction will help you to bear fruit. Come, I need to show you what you have to learn in order to be my disciple."

As they passed more ships, they reached one that looked like a church outside, but inside it looked like a bar. Under the dim light people were dancing to worldly songs. The music was so loud that they didn't seem to hear others crying for help.

Jesus said, "There are quite a few lifeguards on this ship, but they are not concerned with drowning people. I call many to be rescuers, but only a few respond to the need and undertake the extensive training. In order to be rescuers, people have to saturate their hearts and minds with the words of my lifesaving manual and learn about my love and power. Unless they understand my love for them and others and believe my words have the power to save people, they drop out of the course. Even after they finish the training, they have to hold my lifesaving manual in their hearts so that they can tell others about my love. Many put away my book and start carrying a worldly manual written by people influenced by the devil. They deceive themselves by thinking that human reasoning should be placed higher than my lifesaving book. These lifeguards even bring the devil's teaching to my people in the church and say that sinful attitude and behavior is godly. Many stumble and fall because of the fallen leaders of the church. The problem is worse when those fallen lifeguards throw my book of life in the garbage and do not realize that when they do that, they throw themselves in the garbage too. They start living filthy and disgusting sinful lives."

The girl understood why Jesus had brought her there. She said in tears, "Jesus, now I realize that one reason I followed the world and fell into sin was because I didn't hold on to your words. I listened to the worldly standard, not your words. Please forgive me."

"I forgive you, my daughter. When people don't have my words in their hearts, they don't have the power to live godly lives. My words purify people's thoughts, motivations, attitudes, and actions, but I have not given up on these fallen workers. I am still knocking on their doors today, and the Holy Spirit is trying to bring other Christians their way so they hear me and repent. I pray that they will come to an understanding of what kind of spiritual condition they are in and turn to me. When people don't recognize my word as the most powerful life saving book, they start working against me and the Holy Spirit."

"Lord Jesus, how can I know that the Holy Spirit is working in my life? For a long time, I didn't realize that I had to pay close attention to the Holy Spirit's leading."

"My child, the Holy Spirit uses my words to speak to my children in a small voice in their hearts, but many don't understand this and ignore the Holy Spirit. The Holy Spirit lives in you and can guide and comfort you. People don't obey the Holy Spirit because they follow their own desires, instead of what I desire for them. Often, what the Holy Spirit asks them to do is contrary to what people want to do."

"Lord, help me to hear clearly the voice of the Holy Spirit and help me have the courage to do what you are asking of me."

"Unless people start paying attention to my words, they won't be able to hear the Holy Spirit's voice. Remember this: if you look for me earnestly, you will find me. You will be able to hear my voice if you read the Bible and pray diligently and listen to my voice. Still, there are other dangers you need to be aware of. Come, I will show you."

22. The Rescuers

They walked toward the other ships, and she heard loud noises coming from a ship close by. Jesus took her to a ship where a mob of people chased a wounded lifeguard. When the people grabbed the lifeguard, they beat him until the man fell to the floor, then they threw him into the river. A few of Jesus' workers, who were walking on the water, pulled the wounded man onto another ship to help him. Inside the first ship a mob of people was divided into two groups. In one group were the followers of the lifeguard, while in the other were the people who had gotten rid of the lifeguard. They accused each other and started throwing the church furniture at each other. Some fell into the river, but no one noticed.

The girl was shocked. "Jesus, what happened here?"

Jesus replied, "My daughter, many of my workers are accused, stabbed, chased, and beaten by the people in their church. Those who hurt my workers may attend the church, but they belong to Satan. Sometimes even my children are deceived, make wrong judgments, and hurt my workers. I sent my workers to help other Christians rescue drowning people. Too many of my rescuers are discouraged, burned out, and have left the work I gave them. When church people backstab their spiritual leaders, they don't realize that they invite the devil's attack. They are opening their hearts to the devil, who plants seeds of unforgiveness, resentment, and ungodly manners. Sowing bitter seeds in their hearts will choke my people to spiritual death. The devil encourages people to leave the church by telling them that there is no reason to go to a church where there is fighting. Many have listened to the devil's advice, left me, and followed the wide road to destruction. Pray that your church will not fall into temptations like that. Ask my Father to deliver them from evil spirits and to help pull out all the destructive seeds of division in the church. You also need to understand that some spiritual leaders are not working for me but for the devil. I didn't send them but they pretend I called them to do my work. They rely on themselves instead of me. They promote themselves, not me. They use my name to gain others' approval and recognition. In fact, the devil loves these spiritually dead leaders because they help the devil to make more devil's children. You have to rely on me so that you can handle the devil's attacks with my power."

"Lord, what will happen to that lifeguard?"

"Suffering helps a person to have more compassion for others. The more suffering people experience, the more they are able to experience healing power through my words. When my workers recognize that my words can heal their wounds, they can use my medicine to heal other sick people. I am not pleased if my workers decide to listen to themselves and the world. The devil uses that to plant seeds of bitterness, resentment, unforgiveness, and discouragement in their hearts. I grieve if they turn their backs to me. My loving daughter, remember this; you will receive the reward when you run the race all the way and win. Not all of my workers receive a reward because many quit their race. You will grieve me if you quit the race because you can't handle criticism or others' rejection. Don't be discouraged when others misunderstand you. Not all of my children will understand that you are trying to walk with me, because many don't understand other Christians' spiritual walks."

"Jesus, I need your forgiveness. For a long time, I didn't have much respect for the people who work for you. I thought they should work for things they could see. I thought they were foolish to choose a difficult life and poverty. I didn't see much value in following you or working for your kingdom. Please forgive me."

"I forgive you. When people value what they can see, they may have a negative attitude toward my workers. You will meet many people like that when you work for me. I need to warn you about another thing. I will show you what I mean."

They came to a big dark ship. A faint light was coming from the stove burner. Blind and deaf people filled the ship and were drinking coffee. Some blind people fell into the river as they walked along. Others slipped and clung to the edge of the ship, exhausted, crying out for help, but no one came.

"Lord Jesus, why is everyone on this ship blind and deaf? Why do they not have a lifeguard?"

"When people don't believe what I say about eternal hell, they are spiritually blind and spiritually deaf. My children receive rewards according to what they have done when they arrive at my Father's eternal home. Many people, even some of my workers, believe in a heavenly home, but do not believe that there is eternal burning hell for people who reject me. The devil works hard to create distrust in my words, even in my children's hearts, so that they don't look for the lost sheep. When people put their reasoning above my words, the devil paralyzes them to keep them from doing what I want them to do. Many of my children sit on a ship thinking that they are safe, when they don't even know which way to go. Anything contrary to my words, like human wisdom, does not have life but is like a destructive seed that originates from the flesh, the world, and the devil. If there were no eternal punishment and burning hell, why would I suffer and die to save people from their sins?"

The girl cried, "Jesus, please forgive me. I was spiritually blind and spiritually deaf. After you pulled me out of the river, I gave attention only to myself. I forgot that unbelievers would suffer eternally. I was safe, so I thought I didn't have to do anything to save other drowning people."

"Now do you understand why I called you to do my work? Do you understand why I am telling you that the harvest is plentiful but the workers are few?"

"Lord, I didn't realize how many are drowning in the river. How can I be a lifeguard? I don't even know how to swim."

"I will teach you to swim. In order for you to be more

fruitful, you also need to learn how to walk on water by faith. Then you will be able to save more people from drowning."

"How can I walk on the water?"

"In order to walk on the water and save people, you have to transform your mind and heart with my words. Humility is one of the requirements for being able to walk on the water and save people. You need to listen to the Holy Spirit or you will miss opportunities to rescue people. Nothing will be done by your power and wisdom. The Holy Spirit will direct you and give you discernment so that you will understand when, where, how, and to whom to reach out. Remember that you cannot use my power and wisdom to feed your pride, otherwise you will fall after you lead others to God."

"Jesus, please help me to understand what it means to be humble before God."

"My child, when people are not clothed with humility, they cannot walk with me. Proud people cannot find me or see me because they rely on themselves. When you lose sight of me and don't know which way to go, then remember that you have somehow fallen on account of pride. A proud attitude blinds a person's spiritual eyes. When that happens, repent, and find out how you lost the vision of me."

"Lord, for many years, I thought I had strong faith and was spiritually mature, but I was fooling myself. I didn't know where you were. How can I have a humble heart now?"

Jesus said, "In order to walk humbly with me, you have to believe the power of my word and understand how the Holy Spirit works in you. You have to realize that my words are your life-giving spiritual food. Unless you keep reading my words to learn, you won't be able to learn how to be humble. My words have life-transforming power. Many of my workers believe their teaching can change other people's hearts, but without my powerful words as well as the Holy Spirit opening people's hearts to reveal their sins through my words, there will be no repenting, salvation, healing, or transformation. My words are a life-protecting sword to help people fight the enemy of the accusing voice so they can be set free from all the burdens of guilt. My children are called to use the sword to help others in bondage, to set them free by telling them about the message of my love and forgiveness. Some use the sword to cut themselves to pieces by not forgiving themselves and others. You have to recognize that all the glory belongs to God. When you start walking on the water and pulling out drowning people, other people may recognize you as a lifeguard and start appreciating you. Don't give yourself credit but realize that my powerful words and the Holy Spirit have done the mighty saving work. Give glory to God, be humble, and pray, otherwise, you will fall into the sin of pride and be captured by the devil. Many of my workers fall into this trap. My power will not work in people who misuse it to promote themselves. I need humble workers who will use my words for my glory. Now you understand why my words have so much to do with humility."

"Yes, Lord, but my problem is that the more opportunities you provide for me to tell others about your love and the more spiritual insights you give me, the more I have a chance to fall with pride. Even when I try to remind myself to be humble, that also becomes a hindrance; I compare myself with others and think I am more humble than others. I am hopeless; I don't know how you can put up with me."

"When you focus on yourself and compare yourself to others, you fall into a trap of boasting and pride. Keep focusing your mind on me, not on yourself or others."

"Jesus, I still don't understand what humility is."

"Humility is recognizing that the heavenly Father's way is better than yours. Humility is understanding God's will for your life and obeying it with a willing heart. Humility is obeying God even if it causes you pain and suffering. Humility is seeking God's kingdom first. Touch my hands, and learn from me."

The girl touched the holes in Jesus' hands and wept.

"Lord, thank you for dying for my sins. Whenever I forget about the lesson of humility, please let me touch your hands."

23. Commitment

Jesus chose to show love even though it cost his life and his dignity. When people are motivated by love, they willingly take the road of suffering and humility for others. That's the love Jesus was asking of his disciples. That's the love Jesus was asking of her. If she loved Jesus, her sacrifice and difficulties wouldn't stop her from following Jesus. How others would see her was not important. She understood it now.

"My beloved daughter, when you do my work, remember you are not alone. There are others who will be helping you by praying for you. Come, I will show you."

Jesus took her to a town with many churches. Some of them had thick white clouds in straight lines reaching up to heaven. Some had only a few lines of the clouds, and some didn't have any.

The girl asked, "Jesus, I have never seen anything like this. What are those lines of clouds?"

"My child, those are the heavenly phone lines of my people who regularly communicate with my Father in heaven. Praying helps my children fight the spiritual battle and helps them clean out the garbage inside themselves and others. My faithful servants pay attention to my words, follow the Holy Spirit's leading, and use those prayer lines consistently. I am standing with a basketful of heavenly spiritual blessings and am ready to pour them down. My people cannot imagine the things I have prepared for them. They will learn to hear my Father's voice when they start listening to the heavenly phone. The sad thing is that many of my children and my workers have forgotten to call my Father. They think they can handle their lives and my work with their own wisdom and power, but nothing will be accomplished until people have my wisdom."

"Lord Jesus, I am sorry. I only prayed when I wanted something from you or when I was in trouble. I didn't realize that I needed to pray to hear my Father's voice. I didn't pray to receive spiritual blessings, either."

"Many don't expect anything from me because they don't think I can do anything. People don't think I can give them the power to reach out to lost people. Pray that many workers will trust in my power to heal. I have much more to offer my children. When people depend on me to release that power through their prayer, they will see miracles. You will be effective for my kingdom in proportion to how much you depend on my power by praying. I work with people who depend on my power to change lives. Not only do you have to pray to be effective, you also have to be filled with the Holy Spirit. Follow me. I will show you what I mean."

24. Greenhouses

Jesus took her to a town with many greenhouses. Each one had a gardener. Some gardeners had helpers with gardening books that described how to raise sweet plants that would produce more sweet fruits. Some gardeners had more bitter plants, and they had ugly, strange looking animal creatures that brought more bitter plants to grow. Each gardener ate what he or she produced from their own garden and became either sick or healthy.

"Lord Jesus, what is happening here?"

"Each greenhouse represents each person's heart. The plants represent what people are focusing on and to what they give their energy and time. The helper is the Holy Spirit living inside a Christian's heart and helping with my gardening book of life, which explains how to produce good fruits. The little animal creatures are evil spirits who give people advice on how to grow bitter plants, which produce bitter fruits. The bitter plants produce the fruits of the flesh, worldly, unspiritual, sinful desires and actions. People with many bitter plants nurture pride, fear, jealousy, resentment, anger, hate, bitterness, selfishness, unforgiving hearts, and many other destructive attitudes and actions. The sweet trees produce the fruits of the Holy Spirit: humility, joy, godliness, forgiveness, love, hope, faith, unselfishness, faithfulness, perseverance, patience, compassion, thankful hearts, and many other positive attitudes and actions. Carefully watch your thoughts, attitudes, and motives, and see what you are planting, because you will reap exactly what you plant. When you plant bitter plants, you are piling up garbage in your heart. Garbage will burden you and you won't be able to do what I am going to ask of you. In order to pull out the bitter plants and take the garbage out of your life, you need knowledge from the Scripture and the help of the Holy Spirit. You will be filled with the Holy Spirit as you plant sweet plants and produce sweet fruits in your heart. Unless your heart is filled with my words and with the Holy Spirit, you won't be able to do what I am going to ask you to do."

"Now I understand why you asked me to forgive people who hurt me. I didn't realize how much I was nurturing the seeds of an unforgiving heart. Lord, help me to recognize which are bitter seeds and which are sweet seeds. Can you help so I will know what I am planting?"

Jesus said, "I have one thing to tell you. Do you realize that my grace turned you around when you were heading toward the road of destruction?"

"I am sorry, Lord. I thought I was spiritually mature and was seeking you, so I was able to turn myself to you. But I couldn't have turned myself to you if you hadn't spoken to me and called me to do your work. I didn't even realize that I was going the wrong way. I tried to give myself credit instead of recognizing your grace. I am learning that I cannot even trust my own judgments any more. Please forgive my ungrateful heart."

"I always forgive you. I love you so much. I will give you anything, even my life, because I love you."

"I love you Jesus. You already have given your life so that I can be forgiven and live with you in our heavenly Father's home. Thank you so much."

"If I have to do it over again, I would die to save you because I love you, my child."

"Thank you, Jesus. There is no one else like you. You care about me more than anyone else. Help me to hold on to your hand always."

"My daughter, you are worthy of my love. Come, follow me. I have something else to show you."

25. A Country Church

Jesus led her to a country church. Many people were arriving to attend the worship service. Some wore bright, shiny white garments and their faces were bright with big smiles. They were greeting and helping little children so they wouldn't fall.

Jesus' face beamed and he said proudly, "These are my workers. Many of them are not even recognized by others in the church, but I know who they are; they are the pillars of the church."

Others who walked into the church wore dirty, filthy, and ragged garments. They each carried a plate in one hand as if they were ready to go through a cafeteria line. Some carried a sword in the other hand. Some started attacking others with their swords. Some were bleeding and had many cuts. Some carried heavy burdens on their back. Some carried ugly looking evil spirits on top of the burdens on their backs. Some arrived in wheelchairs with others' assistance. All of them carried pouches filled with sweet fruits and bitter fruits. Some shared their fruits with others.

Jesus turned to her and said, "My child, you need to

understand that not all of the people who come to the church are saved. People who repented their sins and washed their sins with my blood wear white robes. People who haven't accepted my word and haven't repented of their sins wear ragged garments."

"Lord, why are there so many wounded people here?"

"My loving daughter, many people are going through the dark valley and along the roads of suffering. Pray that their wounds can be healed quickly, so they can help others who are suffering. My words are powerful medicine for the sick, they give encouragement to the discouraged, lift up the fallen, comfort the troubled, give hope to the hopeless, give help to the helpless, and revive the dying soul. These people come to my feast to feed their hungry souls."

"Why do some have swords and others don't?"

"My words are like spiritual swords. Many of my children are misusing them, are critical and judgmental of others, and fall into the sin of pride. They don't understand that they should use the sword to fight the devil's accusing voices."

"Jesus, why do many still carry burdens on their backs? I thought Christians didn't have to carry burdens because you died on the cross to free us."

"People who carry big burdens have not forgiven themselves or others. Many of my children suffer from the devil's accusing voice in their minds because they don't believe I forgive all of their sins. I call many of my children to serve me, but one of the reasons they don't respond is that they don't know how to forgive themselves. They believe they are not worthy enough to work for me. I don't call people because they are worthy, but because they need me more than others do. Those I call to serve me are the ones that I give more spiritual hunger and thirst and the desire to know me. They can learn from me about my love and power and teach others about me. The devil knows whom I try to call to serve me and he works hard to discourage them from following me. People have to understand that I come to call the sinners. I can use anyone who can accept my forgiveness and respond to my calling because my grace is sufficient for all. I don't even remember their sins anymore. I am still looking for people who can trust me completely and give their lives for revival."

"Lord, what about the devil on some people's backs? They are talking with the devil instead of listening to the Holy Spirit."

"Many are oppressed by the devil because they don't believe Satan exists. People don't have power to resist the devil unless they believe in me and use my name to resist it. Many of my children don't understand the spiritual battle, so the evil spirits hurt them and people think it is a natural cause. My words and the Holy Spirit will help the ones who diligently pray and trust my power. When my people put on the full armor of God, they will be able to win the spiritual battle."

The girl inquired, "What about the pouches? What are they?"

"Everyone carries a fruit pouch full of bitter or sweet fruits. The fruits are what they produce in their own gardens in their hearts. The fruits each person brings to church will determine whether they will build up or hurt the body of Christ. Many are weak and need lots of care because they don't know how to nurture the sweet fruits in their hearts. People who believe in my power to heal will experience healing of the spirit and body. My child, do you understand why I am calling you to serve me?"

"Yes, my Lord, but I feel overwhelmed by the work that needs to be done."

"Start with one person at a time. If you can find one lost sheep and help that person find me, then there will be joy in heaven. My Father will be pleased and there will be a feast because of that one person. Nothing you do for my kingdom is done by your wisdom or power. When you feel overwhelmed, you are not relying on me but yourself. When that happens, stop and pray to receive my wisdom. If you try to do my work with your own wisdom and power, you will fail. You need to pray to receive the power to spread the gospel to the ends of the world. Pray that God will give you the heart to reach out to people who need salvation. Pray that God will open those doors so you will have more opportunities to reach out and bring people to Christ. Pray that you will have revival in your heart. Unless you have revival in your heart, you won't be able to see the differences in other people's hearts when you minister to them. Others will experience revival in their hearts as much as you have experienced it. Follow me."

26. A Forest

Jesus took her to a beautiful forest where colorful trees displayed their glory. It was so beautiful that she felt the glory with all her being. She couldn't believe that a place like this even existed. She ran around the trees, and when she got close to them, she was shocked to find out that the trees were not real, but artificial.

She turned around and asked Jesus, "My Lord, these are not real. If they are not real, how can I feel the beauty and glory in my soul?"

"My daughter, there are many things in life that you will find attractive and beautiful and you can lose your heart to them. That is why many people love things in the world more than me. What you love could be people, or people's wisdom, or manmade things, or things I created. When you fill your heart with those things you don't have any room for me. Whatever fills your heart will become your god. Anything that takes your heart away from me is what you should watch out for."

"Lord, what should I watch out for?"

"My daughter, do you realize that I gave you spiritual

discernment so that you can help the body of Christ? The reason I let you know who is walking with me or who is not walking with me is to help you know for whom you can pray. Instead, you are focusing on yourself and thinking how spiritually mature you are. You are misusing the gift I gave you. You are giving yourself glory. All the glory belongs to me, and when you focus on yourself with a boasting heart, you will lose sight of me."

"Please forgive me, Lord. I didn't even realize that."

"I forgive you. All the beauty in this world will pass away. The beauty you see in this world is only a shadow of heavenly glory. You have to realize that I am the one who gives beauty."

"Jesus, lately I find beauty in other Christians because of their commitment to you and their knowledge about you."

"My child, that's another thing you have to watch out for. You need to learn from other mature Christians, but your focus should be on me. Make sure you don't put others' teaching above my words of life. You need to walk with me and learn from me so you can learn to obey the Holy Spirit's instructions. Come, I have something else to show you."

27. The Heavenly Garden

The girl visited the heavenly garden with Jesus where she felt God's love and beauty in her heart. Until then, she didn't know she could feel love in her heart. The beauty she felt there was something she had never experienced before. The sweet feeling she felt was so overwhelming that she wanted to stay in that garden forever. Reading the Scriptures, praising God by singing hymns, and spending time in prayer brought her more joy than anything. As she walked along the path, suddenly she was standing on a cliff all by herself. Jesus was already on the ground below stretching out his arms and asking her to come down. When she turned around to see the road she had traveled, she was surprised to find it gone. She wanted to stay in the garden longer, but she couldn't.

Jesus called, "My child, it's time for you to come down. I want you to feed others. That's why I have called you."

Reluctantly, she came down, and Jesus helped her to stand on her feet.

Jesus said, "My daughter, you can go back to the heavenly garden when you want, but you cannot stay there all the time. You cannot grow if you only feed yourself. You will grow more when you help others grow spiritually. Your testimony is also my testimony of how I have helped you. It is time for you to go out and tell others how I healed you. Ask me for whatever you want and I will give it to you."

She thought for a moment, then said, "Lord Jesus, all those years I had my own visions, dreams, and hopes of what kind of person I wanted to be and what kind of life I wanted to live. I would like to understand your visions, dreams, and hopes for me. You have been asking me to go out to help others but I don't understand your love for them. I need to understand your love and power so I can reach out to the people you want me to reach."

28. A Hospital

Jesus took her to the town that had a huge hospital full of wounded people. A little girl with one arm cut off, dripping blood, was crying out, trying to find her mother. People around her acted as though they didn't see her or hear her cry. There were a few doctors and nurses busy helping too many people; no one was able to help her.

"Lord Jesus, why don't people help her?" the girl cried.

"My daughter, you are seeing only one of my daughters who is in pain. There are many who are suffering just like her. I need my workers to go out to heal the girl and others. Do you realize that you were like that girl, helpless and in need of an arm?"

"No, I didn't know that," the girl shook her head, tears streaming down her cheeks.

"Look closely at your right arm, the arm you always used to hold on to my hand."

The girl looked closely at her arm and found a scar on her skin. It was as though she had had surgery a long time ago. "What is this scar?" she questioned. "I have never seen this before."

"My daughter, the scar that you are seeing is an emotional scar. I have healed you. I have given you a new arm so that you can hold my hand."

"Thank you, Lord. I didn't even realize that you gave me a new arm. Was the girl that I saw me?"

"Yes. I carried you out of that place in my loving arms. You hurt badly but I healed you. I have the power to heal. Now do you realize why others need to experience my healing power?"

The girl wept. She finally understood why Jesus had come to the world to save suffering people from sin. She also learned that she could not grasp others' suffering unless she experienced it or God granted her the opportunity to taste it, without actually living through it. She was convinced that her decision to follow Jesus to help others was the right one.

"Jesus, how can I help these people? What do you want me to do?"

"Do you remember I told you that we have work to do before we reach our heavenly Father's home?"

"Yes, Lord, what do you want me to do?"

"I am looking for people who I can trust with my power to transform lives. In order to have that power, you have to pay the price."

"What is the price I have to pay?"

Before Jesus answered, a man approached and showed the girl a turnip and explained how much it would cost. "It is $1,400," he said.

She thought if she could plant lots of turnips, she would make lots of money. Suddenly, she found herself standing in a large golden field ready for harvest. If she could plant turnips in that field, she could make lots of money, she said to herself. But there was no time to plow and plant because the field was ready for harvest.

"My daughter, do you remember that I want you to reach out to those in prison because I love them and I have died for them?"

"Yes."

"I am sending you to the prisons, where the field is ready to harvest. You didn't plant. You didn't work hard to make it to that stage, but I am sending you so you can be my worker. Go, I will go with you. I will show you wonders, I will open people's hearts and I will save them. The price you have to pay is to go where I send you. Volunteer to give testimony in different prisons."

She understood then that God had answered her prayers asking for understanding of God's visions, dreams, and hopes for her. She didn't know how God would lead her, but one thing was sure: she could anticipate this harvest with the greatest anticipation she had ever had. God had never failed her or disappointed her. She knew she could bear lots of fruits according to God's wishes. However, that would be the case only if she would pay the price of going to prisons with a willing heart to tell the people about God's love and forgiveness.

"Chile, remember that we are on a journey to our heavenly Father's home. Before we arrive there, we have lots of work to do. Let's help those who need my love and healing. My beloved daughter, do you love me?"

"Yes, my Lord Jesus, I love you."

Jesus said, "If you love me, go out and find my lost sheep, and heal them with my words. I have died on the cross for their sins, and my Father has forgiven them. Tell them they don't have to carry their burdens anymore because I have carried their burdens. Take care of them as I have been taking care of you. Take care of them as you would take care of me."

29. Lost Sheep

Jesus was so powerful. She had seen so many miracles because of Jesus. He not only healed her wounds and her backsliding, he also changed her heart and attitude toward the lost sheep. She understood that she used to be one of the lost sheep. Jesus in his mercy pulled her out of the raging river. Until the Holy Spirit convicted her of her sins, she didn't even realize that she was a sinner. When God helped her to see her pitiful, hopeless, and sinful condition, she realized what was happening. She was carrying a heavy burden of sin. The devil used it to beat her down to the ground and torture her by accusing her of the sins Jesus had paid for on the cross. She cried and asked for God's forgiveness, and God forgave her.

The powerful words of God set her free from all condemnation. All her sins were nailed to the cross when Jesus was nailed to the cross. All of her sins died when Jesus died on the cross. Her spirit came alive with the pure, spotless garment of holiness when Jesus rose from the dead. God had forgiven her and no one could condemn her, not even herself. Jesus' blood washed all of her sins white as snow. She had experienced it.

She understood that whoever believed in Jesus would experience this forgiveness and freedom because God wouldn't remember their sins anymore. There is no condemnation for those who are in Christ because of his sacrificial death on the cross. Because Jesus showed her his love and care when she desperately needed to be free from the burden of sin, she now understood how important it was to reach out to the lost sheep. It would be a terrible sin if she didn't share this wonderful message of forgiveness with others who suffer from the burden of guilt.

Not all the roads she had walked with Jesus were easy.
It was hard for her to understand why Jesus told her that the
road of suffering was the road that she had to follow. While
she was in tears and walking through the thorn bushes with
Jesus, she couldn't understand why Jesus wouldn't lead her to
an easy path.

However, she understood that Jesus didn't create her
misery and suffering. As Jesus told her, she was living in a
fallen world where people are spiritually sick and sinful,
influenced by fallen angels and the devil. Those things
produce suffering. Jesus had love and compassion for
suffering people. Jesus knew what people needed. He
suffered so others wouldn't suffer.

Jesus provided forgiveness, eternal salvation, and
healing, so people could live with perfect joy, peace, comfort,
and freedom in the midst of difficulties and suffering while in
the imperfect world. It was painful for her to follow the roads of
suffering, but the tears and pain helped her to experience
Jesus' healing power, love, and compassion. Through her
suffering, Jesus gave her insight into how others suffer and
need healing.

Some roads she had walked were shameful because
she didn't take Jesus' words seriously. Instead of listening to
Jesus, she listened to herself and the world. She had taken
the road of deception. She had loved the world more than
Jesus. Still, Jesus forgave her and cared for her the whole
way, even when she was not faithful to him. She was snatched
out of the fire. Jesus was the one who pulled her out of a pit
and saved her many times. Jesus' blood washed all of her
shame from the past, present, and future. Jesus' blood has the
power to wash not only her sins, but the sins of all who come
to him and believe in him.

She learned that in order to follow Jesus, she not only
had to let go of worldly desires and things that she enjoyed
before, but she had to change her attitudes and her lifestyle.

She had to change her priorities. Going back to the narrow road was painful because following Jesus required denying her easy way of life. She understood what her cross was and, instead of ignoring that cross, she made a commitment to carry it and follow Jesus.

It was a tearful, long process to follow Jesus, and not many understood why she had to follow him. That thought brought tears because she had to go against people who were very dear to her. She had to make hard choices. She had to evaluate her motivations and reasons for following Jesus. She made up her mind to follow him, not others. That caused tension. She needed that purifying fire to find out how far she was willing to follow Jesus. That fire helped her to see herself better, even though it was painful. Even in the midst of going through the purifying fire, she had experienced Jesus' love, which helped her to understand that God's grace is sufficient in all circumstances.

What Jesus said was true. She didn't belong to this world, but to Jesus. He called her out of the world. For a long time she thought the world was her permanent place to live, but then she learned that was a misconception. As she walked with Jesus, she learned how to say goodbye to every town she passed. As Jesus led her, he had lessons to teach her in different towns, mountains, and deep dark valleys, so that she could be a better servant for God's kingdom. Understanding Jesus became her highest priority, so she started reading the Scriptures more, especially the gospels.

Whenever she thought about how much Jesus loved her and how he had even given his life to save her, her heart was filled with joy and gratitude. Jesus loved her more than anyone else she had met on the road.

Jesus is so loving and powerful. She saw only a glimpse of Jesus' glory, but someday he would lead her to her heavenly Father's eternal home where there is no suffering, no tears, no mourning, no worry, no pain, no sickness, no terror, no despair, no death, no trials, no discouragement, no fears, no disappointment, no backsliding, no heartaches, no temptation, and no deception.

Instead of meeting Jesus in her heart, she will someday be able to see Jesus' loving face and touch him and tell him how much she loves him. She has been thinking about what she wants to do when she sees Jesus face to face. She will fall down to worship him, and hold on to his right leg, thanking him for walking with her and saving her from all the dangers during her life. Until then, she knows what she has to do. Her duty is to tell others how much Jesus loved her and forgave her, so others can understand how much Jesus loves them and forgives their sins. She learned that there are too many lost sheep in the world. Jesus is the only one who can save people and give them hope.

The girl understands what will happen when she obeys the Holy Spirit: Jesus will go out with her to search for the lost sheep. Jesus will carry the lost sheep in his arms. Jesus will heal and take care of the wounded sheep. Jesus will help her to take care of the lost sheep with God's love and power. Jesus will always walk with her and tell her that he loves her. Jesus will lead her to the heavenly Father's home safely. Jesus will happily welcome her when she arrives at the heavenly Father's home.

Part Three:
A Prayer of Blessing

I pray that you will be blessed
and experience Jesus every moment,
so that you will hear His voice clearly,
see His compassionate face,
feel His gentle arms carrying you,
understand His urgent calling,
follow Him immediately to serve Him,
love Him with all your being,
give Him all you have,
obey Him till death,
see His glory,
and experience healing.

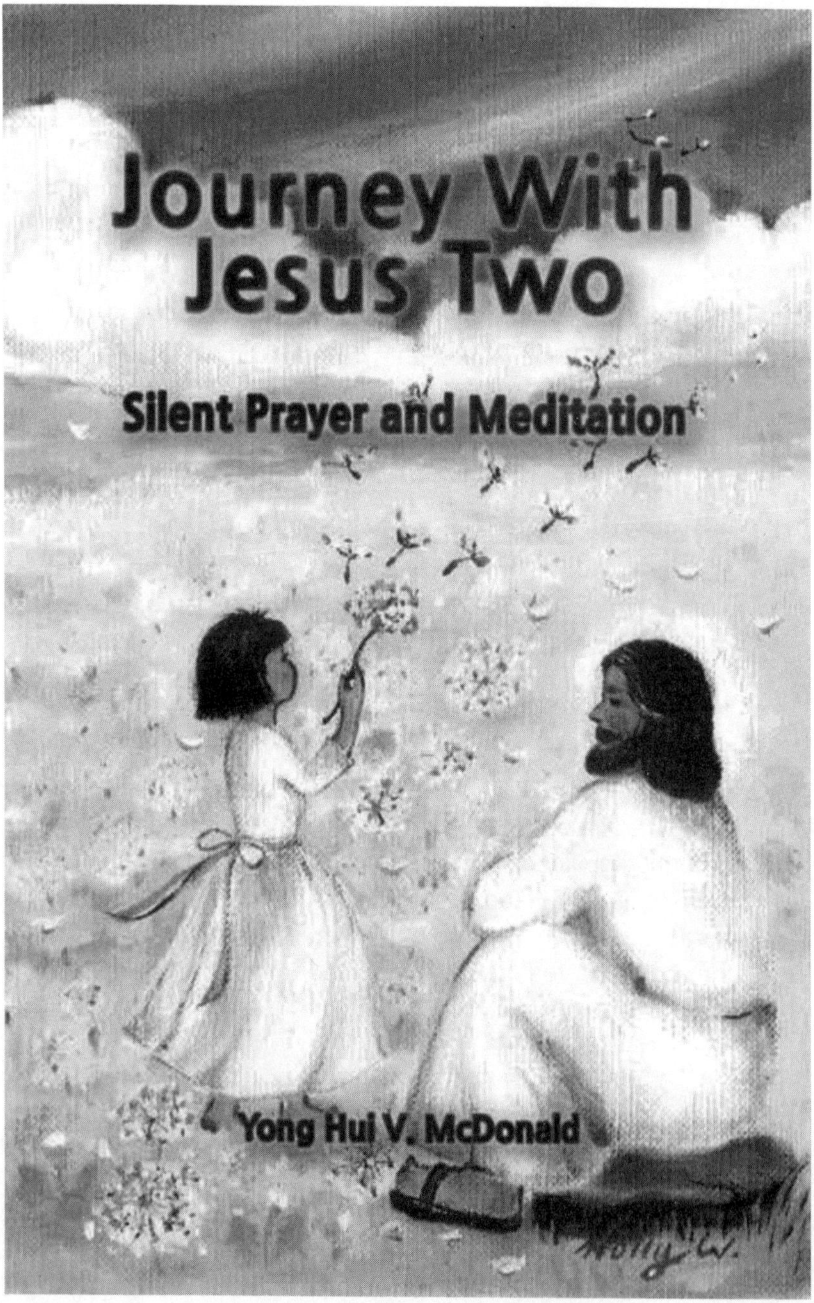
Journey With Jesus Two
Silent Prayer and Meditation
Yong Hui V. McDonald

INTRODUCTION

I ran away like Jonah when the Lord first called me to the ministry. However, as I was writing *Journey With Jesus*, the Lord changed my heart. I felt Jesus' love and His love for the lost when I finally realized that all I had to do was rely on the Holy Spirit's power when I followed His call into the ministry.

God called me to the prison ministry and I started working as a chaplain at Adams County Detention Facility in 2003. I have experienced revival through Transformation Project Prison Ministry (TPPM), a non-profit organization that publishes and distributes books to prisons and homeless shelters free of charge.

I was blessed with lots of ministry projects, but as I got busy I neglected time with the Lord. He called me to silent prayer on December 8, 2013, and helped me to write *Journey With Jesus Two*. This second book brought significant changes to my prayer life. I had to learn to listen to God in silence and follow His direction. I praise Jesus for leading me to write this book and thank Him for teaching me the importance of listening to His voice in silence.

Part One:
Journey With Jesus Two

1. A Flower Bed

After the girl decided to follow Jesus, she began to feed many starving souls with books the Lord guided her to produce. She found so much joy! She witnessed the revival she yearned to see through prison ministry and book projects.

The girl had seen many miracles along the road, including Jesus healing the sick and feeding thousands of hungry people with only a few pieces of bread. She felt very grateful that he had called her to witness this amazing power of God.

The journey continued when the Lord took her to a valley that was carpeted with dandelions. This was the most breathtaking sight she had ever seen. She ran and ran through the flowers. Everywhere she looked there were gorgeous yellow blooms moving gently with the breeze. She jumped to see more flowers, then ran around and found a spot to lie down and look at the clear blue sky. The girl felt like she was in heaven.

The flowers gently touched her face. She had never thought that such a place existed. Dandelions are considered weeds in the lawn, but in this valley they seemed to be singing along with the birds. Each flower she looked at seemed to be speaking to her, and she forgot about the Lord who had brought her there. While she was holding the flowers and admiring them, she felt the beauty of the place with her whole

being. She started blowing dandelion seeds into the air and felt overwhelmed by all the beauty that surrounded her.

Jesus watched her for a while, then tapped her shoulder gently to get her attention.

"My loving daughter, I have answered your prayer. You wanted to see a revival, so I brought you to a place where you could witness one. Prison is where a revival is happening and you are in the midst of it. You will be filled with joy because of it, but I need to ask you a question."

The girl kept blowing the seeds, lost in the beauty of them. She didn't even look at Jesus when she said, "What is it, Lord?"

Jesus sat by her and glanced at her. "My daughter, the time has come for you to make a decision. Which do you love more, me or the flowers?"

The girl was not paying attention to him. She kept jumping in the flower bed and lying down to look at the side view of the flowers. She said, "Lord, you brought me here to enjoy these flowers. I'm just so happy here! This is a beautiful place."

Jesus said, "My daughter, I want you to pay attention to my word. You have to make a decision. You can't love the flowers that you see and love me at the same time. You must decide. Which do you love more, me or the flowers?"

The girl sat up and thought about it for a while. She realized that she misunderstood her journey. Her journey with Jesus was the most important thing in her life. The valley Jesus had brought her to was just a place to rest for a while. She was so captivated by the beauty of the flowers that she forgot about her journey. Prison ministry gave her abundant joy because she was dedicated to serving Jesus. However, as time passed, she had focused more on the ministry than following him.

The girl got up from the flower bed and said, "Jesus, I am sorry. I forgot about our journey. You are the most important person in my life. These flowers are only here for a short time, then they will disappear. When we passed through the garden, I totally forgot about you. Of course I choose to love you more than the flowers."

Jesus said, "There you go, you made the right decision. I love you daughter. I love you more than my life." Jesus took her hands and his eyes were filled with love. He swung her around and made her feel loved. Everything looked beautiful and she knew that the flowers were temporary but the Lord is eternal. Jesus is the one who satisfies her soul and takes care of her during difficult times. Now he reminded her of the journey that was ahead of her.

The girl said, "Lord, I will never forget you. Thank you for reminding me that you are the one who brought me to this place and let me enjoy the beautiful flower bed. I want to stay here forever."

"My daughter, there are many more places I need to show you. You are just passing through this place. It is temporary. When we get to our Father's home, that will be permanent."

"Can I stay here just a little longer?"

"No, it's time for us to move on to another place. There are many more places you need to visit before we arrive at our Father's home."

The girl reluctantly turned from the flowers and began to follow Jesus.

2. A Stone of Plans

As she walked the girl started playing with a little polished stone that she hid in her hands. The little stone had traveled with her for many years. She loved this stone because it had shiny sparkles in it. Whenever she turned it to different angles, she could see it shine and sparkle brightly. She was amazed by the beauty of the stone. It was so small that when she held it no one else could see it, not even Jesus. Well, that's what she thought. She decided that the stone could be her little secret that Jesus didn't need to know about.

Jesus knew everything. He noticed her playing with the stone but he didn't say anything. Then one day, when she got caught playing with her stone, she quickly hid it from him.

Why? It seemed to her that Jesus always wanted whatever she had, and this was the one thing that she thought she could keep. Before, she used to have a lot of stones, but Jesus had told her that his workers couldn't carry anything because they became a burden. However, she didn't think having this little one stone could hurt.

Jesus quietly stood there looking at her. He shook his head. "My loving child, why won't you give me your stone?"

She squeezed her hands tightly. For the first time she realized how much she treasured this stone.

"Jesus, I gave you all the other stones. I would like to keep this one. I love to play with it and it's not too heavy to carry."

"Do you know what that stone represents?" Jesus asked.

The girl opened her eyes wide. The stone didn't have anything written on it before, but now she could see engraved words which she had missed.

She said, "Lord, it says 'my future plans.'"

"I want you to put your future plans in my hands."

"Jesus, I have been making my future plans so that I can serve you."

"My child, you misunderstood what it really meant to follow me. You can't have your own plans when you decide to follow me. As long as you have that stone, you can't do what

95

I want you to do. That's like my disciples telling me that they will follow me, as long as my plans line up with their own.
I have plans for you. If you have your own plans, you can't follow me where I am going. You have to give me the stone and let me decide where I want you to go."

Jesus' stern look surprised her. He stood there waiting.

The girl didn't want to give it up. "Lord, why do I have to give you my plans for the future? Didn't I give you enough? Didn't I sacrifice my life to follow you?"

"My loving daughter, you have shown me your love. All my workers have to give me everything they carry, including their future plans, so that I can guide them to do my work according to my will. If you have your own plans, even if you are doing good things, you will be serving yourself instead of me."

"Jesus, I didn't realize how tightly I was holding this stone. I thought that as long as I had plans to serve you, that would be enough. Why am I having a difficult time giving it up?"

"You don't completely trust what I can do with your life. Also, you don't see the big picture I see. I see a great kingdom building project, but I need the right workers in the right places in order to complete the project."

"I am sorry, Lord. I didn't know that I wasn't completely trusting you. I know that your plans are always better than mine. You called me to prison ministry. What's wrong with making plans to continuously work with prisoners until I die?"

"There is nothing wrong with it. But I also want you to reach out to leaders outside of prison, not just locally, but internationally, so you can train them."

"I thought I was training the leaders inside of prison."

"Yes, you are, and you will continue training them through many more books. However, you have to make up your mind how you will serve me. You don't know how I am going to use you in the future. I want to direct you so that you can do what I want you to do."

"Jesus, don't you think that I am doing enough?"

"Most of the time, you don't even understand what your gifts are. I'm only asking you to give me your stone so that I can lead you where I want you to minister. You only think about your own comfort when you have your own plans. When you do that, you ignore my plans for you."

"Lord, I didn't realize that I was making my own future plans only to keep myself comfortable. I finally realize that I have been ignoring the Holy Spirit because I didn't want to do what he was asking me to do. I was telling you what I thought I should be doing instead of listening to you tell me what I should do. Please forgive me. Here is the stone."

The girl finally gave the stone to Jesus.

He smiled at her. "My child, you have given me your life, but it's not a complete submission until you have given me your plans. You have finally given me what I wanted from you. I will share my plans with you. I am going to lead you to reach out to many people so that you can be more effective in serving me. I have been training you to be able to write this book. Be prepared. I will give you directions soon. You need to obey the Holy Spirit's leading. I am teaching you how to be obedient. As long as you are obedient to the Holy Spirit, it will not be difficult for you to follow me. I want you to be prepared because I don't want you to struggle when I ask you to do something for me."

The girl said, "Lord, why is it so hard to give you everything?"

"You don't spend enough time with me, so you don't understand my heart."

"Help me to spend more time with you so I don't have surprises."

"I will be training you to listen so you can obey my directions."

The girl was happy and started dancing. The sun was bright and the mountains seemed to be dancing with her in the reflection of the river. Her dancing pleased Jesus. He clapped his hands and smiled, then started skipping and dancing with her.

3. Silent Prayer

The girl was busy feeding spiritually hungry people. She always seemed to be happy listening to inspirational music and there wasn't much time in her busy schedule to spend with Jesus.

One day, the Holy Spirit asked her to spend more time listening to the Lord. She began to call this a time for "Silent Prayer." At first, it seemed impossible for her to stop everything to be with only Jesus. She kept postponing this call to silent prayer; she poured all her time and energy into her ministry instead.

Eventually, this request from the Holy Spirit for silent prayer became very urgent. She realized that she was getting sick and needed healing from the Lord.

It was on December 8, 2013, that Jesus said, "My loving child, I want you to spend time with me. You are too busy to understand my heart. That's why you need to spend time in silent prayer, waiting for me to speak to you. I want you to stop talking to others as much as possible. Turn the music down completely. If you want to understand my heart, you need to curtail your other activities as much as you are able so that you can listen and be healed."

This was around the time that she had finished the English version of the book *Loving God* and was working on the Korean version. The book teaches others how to love God. It was also an assignment the Lord had given her. It seemed ironic that she was trying to teach others to put their time aside to love him, but lacked in this area herself. The Lord wanted

her to practice loving God by listening in silence to his voice while in his presence.

She felt sick, so she didn't have any choice but to obey him. She stopped listening to hymns and told others that she had to spend more time in silence with the Lord in order to focus on listening to Jesus. Some people didn't understand her and still wanted to talk to her. She almost explained it to them again, but the Lord told her not to. He gave her Paul's words to the churches in Galatia: "Am I now trying to win the approval of men, or of God? Or am I trying to please men? If I were still trying to please men, I would not be a servant of Christ." (Galatians 1:10) This gave her the courage to focus on just praying, since that's what the Lord wanted her to do.

"My daughter, if you spend so much of your time healing others, you don't have the time to be healed. I have many lessons to teach you, which will help you understand your spiritual condition. I will heal you. You need my strength to be healed. Come and follow me. I have many things to show you."

4. A Heart of Stone

As they walked along the road, it was quiet, except for the birds singing in the air. She kept listening, as Jesus wanted her to. He said nothing for a long time. The girl was wondering why the Lord had asked her to be silent. She still didn't know.

The first week the Lord walked with her, he shared his concern about children living in poverty. He said, "My loving child, I want you to work on children's books. There are many who are so poor that their parents can't buy books for them. If you plant the seed of my love in children's hearts, they will be able to understand my love. They will be saved and they will walk with me."

Up until then, the girl had only written books for adults so she said, "I will work on it Lord."

"It's very important to reach out to the poor. Many children are on the streets and they need to hear my loving word. You need to expand your ministry."

"I will try to do that, Lord."

The girl continued to follow Jesus. She remained silent, since that's what he wanted. They walked in silence for three weeks. As they were passing by the mountain, Jesus spotted some green grass and he sat down. She sat beside him. This time he had something in his hands. When he opened them, she saw a little stone inside a paper. The stone was polished a pinkish color. She grabbed it and even though it had rounded sides, it felt rough. "Why are you showing me this stone?"

"My daughter, I can break the hearts of stone and turn them into flesh."

"Jesus, you are amazing! I knew you could do it."

"My child, that's what I did with you. Your heart was getting hardened like stone, but in my mercy I poured out my

love for you. My love, my tears, and my blood poured out for you because I love you."

"Yes, Jesus, I know that you love me."

"My loving daughter, when I picked you up, you were in pain. Your heart was hardened like a rock by the harsh environment you were in. I poured out my love for you and your heart was melted, turned to living life. Since you believe in me, you have the desire to know my love and you have love for me. I have shown you that my love is the only thing that can sustain your life and keep you from falling into disappointment, discouragement, and despair. I have offered you everything you need to live a happy life. My love will heal your broken heart, take away your pain, and fill you with peace and joy."

The girl's face glowed. "Thank you, Jesus, for giving me life. It's by your grace that I understand your love. I want to have more love for you."

"My beloved daughter, I can do all these things, but I need my workers to tell others about my love for them so that their hearts will turn to flesh and fill with my living life."

"Jesus, how can I teach this to others?"

"Write another *Journey With Jesus* book for others to understand my love for them. This will open and melt their hearts of stone."

"Really? You want me to write another *Journey With Jesus*?"

"Yes, it's going to reach out to many people. This time, your deep love for me has to be the focus, because I delight in my children's love."

"My Lord, I feel inadequate to tell the world of my deep love for you. You know how easy it is for me to forget about you when I am distracted."

"My loving daughter, that's your understanding, but my understanding is different than yours. Your desire to love me is what I want from others. In order to do that, I want you to teach others about my love for them and my desire to have an intimate relationship with them."

"Lord Jesus, how can I teach others how to love you?"

"Until people learn to be satisfied with my love, they will not really learn. Tell others how I have shown you my love as we walk together. You were tempted to follow the world, but you decided to follow me. Others opposed your decision to follow me, but you followed me anyway. You faced rejection from your family and others, as well as many other obstacles, when you decided to obey me. You sacrificed your comfort and followed me. I saw your tears. I will bless you for your obedience."

"Thank you, Lord, but you didn't give me much choice. The Holy Spirit's urging was so great that I had to obey you. As I look back, I am glad that I decided to follow you instead of other people."

"My beloved daughter, I have a reason to call you to do this. I have great plans for you to reach out to others who feel that no one loves them. People feel lonely, but nothing can make them happy. They can't be happy with anyone or anything but my loving presence. You learn about my love and presence when you walk with me. Ask me any questions that puzzle you. I will answer you so that you can start writing this book."

"Lord, I feel like I have too many book projects, but since you asked me, I will write it. How can I start?"

"Start with the story of the stone and what I have shown you in your prayers. I will give you what you need to write. You don't have to worry. I only give you assignments that you can do. I will be with you and all your other book projects because they help many spiritually hungry people."

"Jesus, I remember I asked you if you would help me write about your heart. Now, you are giving me another assignment to share about it. Thank you, Lord, for the direction. I thought I was finished with the *Journey With Jesus* story. When I wrote that book, it changed my life and helped me make the decision to go into the ministry."

"My daughter, as long as my journey continues with you, the story is not finished. I will help you write it. You need to remember that unless you spend time in silence before me, you can't understand my heart. I am also answering your prayers. You said you wanted to write another book like *Journey With Jesus*. This book will be your loving journey with me. Your story will tell others how much I love them. It will be for my glory and glory to the Father. The Holy Spirit will help you with this book."

"Thank you, Lord Jesus, for letting me know your heart. Thank you for the assignment and your guidance."

5. A Sick Man

Jesus said, "My loving child, come, follow me. I want to show you something."

Jesus took her to a busy market. There was a sick man lying on a stretcher. He seemed to be so weak that he couldn't move. His eyes were shut and it was hard to tell if he was breathing or not. The girl wondered if he was dead. He was waiting for an ambulance to take him to the hospital.

The girl said, "Lord, who is this man?"

Jesus answered, "This man is one of my workers. He is a spiritual leader. Sadly, many of my workers are sick and dying. They are in desperate need of my care."

"Why, Lord? Why don't you just heal him as you have done with many others? I know you can raise the dead. You did that with me. My soul came alive when you poured your love into my heart of stone."

"I can't when they don't turn to me for healing. They don't understand my power and love. My daughter, before I called you to silent prayer, your spiritual condition was like this man's. You had been so busy with ministry that you were not spending time with me. You didn't even realize how sick you were. You didn't seek my love and presence to heal you. You relied on your own strength for too long. When you don't look up to me and spend time with me, you will get sick like that man. I saw you lying on a stretcher like that and I grieved for you. I was praying for you to turn to me and be healed."

The girl started crying. She had been exhausted and couldn't figure out why. She thought that she was catching a cold and needed medicine. As time passed, she realized that her fatigue was not from physical problems but from her soul. She began to wonder if that was what others called 'burn out.'

She thought she could continue to do all the work required for ministry, but there were times she felt she couldn't complete a simple task like she used to. Why did it seem like

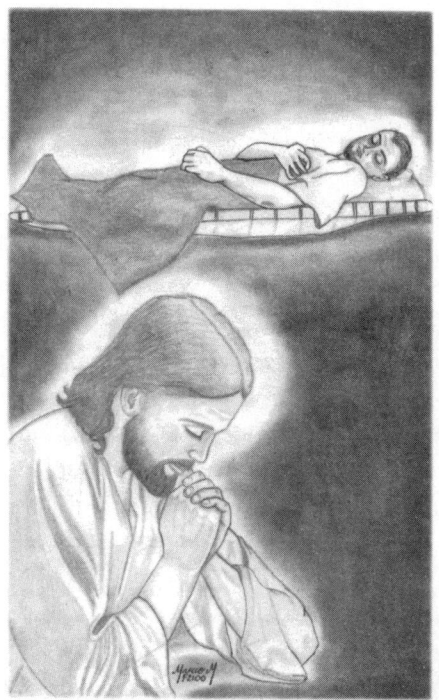

an overwhelming task? She had to ask others to help her. It was the Lord's plan to heal her from spiritual sickness by telling her to look up to him. Jesus knew how to cure her from spiritual exhaustion. She needed to spend time with him in silent prayer.

If this is what's happening to other spiritual leaders, this could be a dangerous situation. People get overworked in the name of God because they don't seek time to rest in the Lord. That's what had happened to her.

She said, "I'm sorry Lord. I didn't know my spiritual condition. I thought everything was going well. Many people are fed because of the books you helped me write. We were able to publish many books and help a lot of people, but I ran out of spiritual energy."

105

"My loving daughter, what you did was fine because you were following the Holy Spirit's lead. However, if you had spent time with me while you were doing the ministry, you wouldn't have felt run down. Your ministry took so much of your time that you relied on yourself and other people for strength more than me. You need to have my strength to do my work. You need to be fed by me. You need to hear my loving words. That's the reason why I called you to pray more and to limit the time you spend conversing with others. You can't mentor others if you are not fed by me first. That's what you have been doing. In the end, you have nothing to give to others. That's why I asked you to stop mentoring because you need my care before you can help others. Also, when you spend too much time with others, you become a hindrance to their spiritual growth. You have to encourage them to spend more time with me. What you don't understand is that they need me more than they need you. That's why you need to remind them."

"I'm sorry Lord. Please forgive me. I was not doing what I was supposed to be doing—reminding them to look to you more."

"I grieve when many of my workers are in the hospital on stretchers, because sometimes no one can help them. People don't understand what's happening to them."

"My Lord, what should I do?"

"Child, I wanted you to spend more time with me so that you could be healed. I called you to help other spiritual leaders, but how can you help others if you are sick? From now on, don't speak to anyone more than you speak to me. Don't allow anyone to be closer to you than I am. This is a warning for you and to other workers. You can't have the strength to help others until you have been healed and strengthened by me. You will be healed as you wait in silence before me and listen to my voice. You need to be healed by my loving words and my presence. The Holy Spirit has been telling you to pray more, but you didn't listen to him."

The girl cried, "Lord, help me so that I don't get sick anymore. I didn't realize I can't minister to others with my own strength. I had nothing to give to others when I was ignoring you."

"My loving daughter, do you see why I brought you here? To show you your spiritual condition."

The girl cried, "Now, I am learning that even good things can be a hindrance between you and me. When I try to do ministry with my own strength, I run out of energy. I feel like I have no strength left. Help me not to let anyone or anything come between you and me."

"I need to warn you that sometimes people will admire you, but that's because of what I have shared with you. If you focus on seeking other people's love and approval, you work for yourself instead of me. Your job is to direct them to me so that they can spend more time with me. I don't want you to become a hindrance to other people's spiritual growth. I am telling this to all the spiritual leaders who are gathering people for themselves instead of teaching them to look up to me."

"Lord Jesus, please forgive me and help me not to seek people's love and approval. What I need is your love and approval instead."

"My loving daughter, it's important to learn that I am the one who fills all of your needs."

"Thank you, Lord, for reminding me of that. You met all my needs when I was walking through the wilderness. You fed me and gave me something to drink. Help me to remember that you are the one who blessed me with all the good things in life."

Jesus smiled. "I am so glad that you remember that. Come and follow me. I have many things to teach you."

6. Remember Me

This time, Jesus took her to an empty church where he taught her about what he did for her. He walked to the altar and said, "My precious daughter, I want you to remember what I have done for you. Do you remember how I showed you love?"

"My Lord, I remember that you died on the cross for my sins. You gave your life to save me from sin and eternal hell."

"My loving daughter, I want you to remember what I have done for you whenever you are feeling down. I want you to meditate on what I did in order to restore your soul."

Jesus took the bread and said, "My daughter, this is my body which is given for you. I want you to know that the reason I died on the cross was to free you from sin and death. I want to share this with you." Jesus gave her the bread and she took it and ate it. Jesus said, "Here is my cup. I want you to remember that I shed my blood for you, so that you can be forgiven."

"Lord, how can I love you with all my heart, mind, soul, and strength? You gave me your life. I want to give you mine."

"Until people understand my love for them, they can't love me. That's why I called you to silent prayer—for you to understand my love for you. That's what my workers are assigned to do. Unfortunately, many of my workers are busy pleasing people and they are not working for me. They can do many good things, but they don't turn to me to understand my love for them. They don't know how to love me so they can't teach others how to love me."

"Lord, I am sorry that I was not a good example for others of how to love you."

"My daughter, that's why I am teaching you about my love. Before, you didn't know how much I loved you, but now, you begin to understand it. I want you to understand my deep love so you can share it with others."

"Please teach me. I want to learn about your deep, passionate love for me."

"You need to read the Bible more and continue with this silent prayer. I will show you my deep love and how you need to teach others. It's easy for my workers to fall into the trap of trying to please people more than me."

The girl wiped her tears and said, "Lord, why is it so hard to learn the lesson of how to love you? I thought loving my ministry was loving you."

"My loving daughter, many of my workers have forgotten that their ministry is not for them but for me. That's what makes them spiritually sick—they are not fed by me. They starve from a lack of time spent with me. You need to teach them how to love me so they can be healed. You are one of my workers and that's what you need to do."

"Lord Jesus, I am sorry. Please forgive me for loving my ministry more than you."

"I knew that you didn't know what was going on. I forgive you. Teach my workers to gather people for my name's sake."

"Jesus, teach me how to do that."

"I want you to experience my love for you as you take communion in remembrance of me."

She had led Holy Communion in worship many times, as well as doing communion at home. This time, she noticed that the Korean translation started "On the night the Lord was arrested," but the English translation says, "On the night when he was betrayed." There is a big difference between the two translations.

The Korean translation touched her so much that she had a difficult time meditating on the words. Jesus was arrested for her because he loved her. Is there anyone who would willingly be arrested on her behalf and die for her sins? No one would do that, yet the Lord Jesus had done it for her. This communion meditation continued for many weeks. She felt the presence of the Lord so strongly that she choked with tears. Why was it so touching this time? It was the Lord's plan to teach her about his love for her. Jesus' body was broken because he loved her and his blood was shed to forgive her. This love and grace is what she had felt. Who could love her like Jesus? No one but him. She felt so much gratitude. She looked up to Jesus to thank him.

"Lord Jesus, how can you love me so much?"

The Lord smiled. "My loving daughter, you will understand more as you walk with me. I love you more than my life."

"Now I finally understand why you stopped me and asked me to pray in silence. You wanted me to listen to you. I was dying spiritually and I didn't even realize it. I was not able to help others in that condition. Thank you so much for your love. My ministry was taking so much time away from you. Help me not to do that anymore. Now, I know that you are the only one who can heal me."

"There are many people in this market, but how many of them are searching for me? How many are trying to show me their love? How many are trying to tell others about my love? The harvest is plentiful but the workers are few. If my workers are just satisfied with harvesting and forget about me, then they become spiritually sick. They can only be strong when they have a close relationship with me. If you are continuously telling others about how much I love them, then there will be more revival. There will be a great revival if my workers are healed in my presence. I can't wait to see a great revival for my own kingdom's sake. Many of my workers in the harvest field are just happy to see results and they don't pay attention to their own spiritual health. They forget that I want them to turn to me for strength and direction. Many have forgotten why I called them because they focus on their own plans more than mine."

7. The Candle

This time, Jesus took her to a remote town where the only light was a tiny moon. The town was big but seemed strange, as all the lights were off. The girl was used to seeing many beautiful lights in different towns at night, but it felt like there was no life in this town because there were no lights.

She asked, "Lord, did the electricity go out in this town? Why is there so much darkness?"

"My daughter, that's why I brought you here. I have many workers in this town to generate power, but they are sleeping instead of paying attention to people's needs. Not only have they run out of power, but they have rejected the Holy Spirit's power in their lives as well. Many have burned their candles out and all the lights have gone off. They don't have anything left to give. Many have relied on other people and things, instead of on me."

"Lord Jesus, why is it so hard to recognize that you give them light and the right path to follow?"

"That's because many of my workers are not paying attention to me. Those workers have responded to my call but haven't continued to listen to my word. Instead, they replaced it with their own knowledge and understanding, which doesn't have light. There is no life in people's wisdom. A person's wise words can't save others. Only my powerful words can save people and set them free from the devil."

"What do you think I should do, Lord?"

"Keep praying that you will be able to reach out to them. What so many people don't understand is that I am the one who gives light. They don't realize that I am their Lord and Savior who can save them from eternal fire."

"Oh Lord, help me to reach out to them so they can meet you as their Lord and Savior."

"I am grieving for the people who are lost and in pain but don't know how to find me. My workers are supposed to be there to help them find me so that they can be healed. Spread my word. My word is light to their souls."

"Help me to help them, Lord."

8. The Prayer Line

Jesus took her to a war zone, where many of Jesus' workers had shut off the prayer phone line and fallen asleep. Some houses were already invaded by the enemy, but the leaders were sleeping and unaware of the situation. Some of the leaders were taken captive by the enemy and put in prison for greed and lust. They said that it's no use to serve the Lord.

Jesus looked really sad. He said, "My loving child, these are my workers, but many have been taken captive by the enemy. They didn't listen to me, my word, the Holy Spirit, or other people's warnings, and they kept heading toward their destruction. Their lives are filled with misery and torment because the devil has fooled them by telling them it is alright to live in sin. What they don't realize is that living in sin makes them spiritually weak. They can end up working for the enemy if they don't repent. It's all because they didn't pay attention to my living words, which purify their thoughts. If they don't repent, they will be taken as prisoners by the devil and tortured in eternal hell. The pain they will feel will be much greater than what they are feeling now. Repenting will release them from that prison of torture. I always forgive those who repent and ask for forgiveness."

"My Lord, I am sorry that I don't always pay attention to your word or pray diligently. I am so glad that you called me to pray in silence so that I can listen to you now. I didn't realize that I was the one who sometimes shut the communication line off and did whatever I thought I had to do for you instead of what you wanted. I didn't realize that it was grieving you greatly."

Jesus looked at her eyes and said, "My loving daughter, I want to warn the leaders who depend on their own understanding and not on my word. My words can break the heart of stone. My words can convict sins. My words can save people. My words can give people hope. My words can give them spiritual direction. My words can give them the power to win against temptation. My words will purify anyone who repents. My words can heal a broken heart. My words can raise the dead. Many don't know this. You need to remind them."

The girl replied, "Lord, how can I do it? It seems like everyone, especially the leaders, already know the power of words. I wouldn't be telling them anything new. I am not sure if they will listen to me. This task seems to be too big for me. How can I tell others about what you are telling me when people think they already know what I am saying?"

"My loving child, people who are at war need to listen to their commander. I am that commander, and I am telling them to pay attention to my word. You need to tell others, whether they listen to you or not. That's your job. You need to remind

them of what I am telling you. If only one person listens to you, it's worth the effort. I don't want that one person to be in torture and to suffer in eternal hell."

The girl said, "Lord Jesus, whatever I do, if it will help only one person, help me to do it. You told me to write a book. If that will help just one person, I will do it."

Jesus said, "Now you understand my heart. You need to save the lost sheep. Look for the lost sheep in the wilderness, where the wolves are searching to find food. Many have already been taken by the wolves to be eaten. The cries from those who have shut down their prayer lines are not heard. You need to tell them that I died for their sins and that they are forgiven. Many of my workers had so many distractions that they forgot to turn their prayer phone lines to me. This is the condition of many who are working for my kingdom."

The girl cried. "Lord Jesus, I am so sorry. I should use that prayer line more often, that way I understand what's happening in the spiritual war."

"There are many up in the front and they don't know how much they have been attacked. They think everything is going fine in their own eyes. Unfortunately, I see my lost sheep eaten by the wolves, but these leaders don't help them."

"My Lord, I am sorry. I didn't realize that. Let me know what's happening so I can obey you and do what you want me to do."

"My loving child, I want you to be careful when people praise you for the books you have written. The problem is that you can feel satisfied with victories in small areas and forget that there are many others who still need to hear the message of the gospel. Those books have to be distributed in the places where many are suffering from the wolves' attacks. They need to hear the message that I can save them with my loving words from the hurts and attacks caused by the wolves. People need to learn to fight the spiritual battle."

"Lord, teach me how to go about it."

"Find the leaders and train them. That's the only way you can carry out what I want you to do. Find leaders who have the same heart for lost sheep. If you work with leaders who have the same heart to reach out to the lost sheep, train them to draw their strength from me. I see the tears of my lost sheep even now. They don't know how they can find peace and relief from the enemy's attack and torture."

"Jesus, forgive me for my lack of understanding. Please forgive me for not paying attention to the suffering of many who are lost. Let me have your wisdom and heart to be able to reach out to the leaders who can fight this battle with me. Send many leaders who can join in this battle, so together we can save many lost sheep."

Jesus looked pleased. "Now you're getting it. You can't do it alone. You need other workers to fight the battle with you

so that many more lost sheep can be found. That's why I asked you to reach out to children. When you start early, they will be more open to my words. You see why I asked you to train the leaders from the beginning of your ministry. When you work with leaders who have the same heart, you can reach out to many people. Come and follow me. I have many more things to show you."

9. A Gift Basket

As they walked along, Jesus had a basket full of gifts wrapped with brown paper. All the gift boxes were the same size.

The girl asked, "Lord, what's in the boxes?"

"My loving child, I am always prepared to give gifts to my children who come to me to pray and seek my face. I give these gifts to those who purify themselves and come to me so that they will be strengthened for the glory of my Father. Unfortunately, many don't know about this. I want you to tell others that the gift I give them will strengthen their faith and give them direction. The Holy Spirit will direct their use of

117

these gifts. You will learn about these gifts as you wait in silence. You will open the gifts when I give them to you."

"Lord, please bless me with patience so I can wait in silence. Bless me with gifts so that I can love you and serve you."

10. Dirty Water

Jesus took her to a town that had a river as well as a big sewer. Many people were throwing good things into the river. There was lots of stuff in the dirty water. Some of it was good, but it was quickly sucked into the sewer.

"Lord, what are you trying to teach me with this?"

Jesus turned to her and said, "Many people are reading the Bible, but since they are not applying it to their lives, their lives are sucked into the dirty world. Loving the world is like that. Only when they repent and obey my words can they be saved from disaster."

"Lord, why is it so hard to obey your words?"

"Come, let me show you something else."

Jesus took her to a little pool where a clear plastic container that held a message of God's words was floating. The lid was shut but water had started leaking in.

"What is it, Lord?"

"My loving daughter, that container has the word of God in it. People put the word of God in a container. It has a message of how to fight the spiritual battle, but they don't pay any attention. They put it in a safe place instead of utilizing the knowledge they have learned. They don't keep the words in their heart, but save it in a safe container and put it away. My word has to be engraved in their hearts so they can understand my love."

The girl said, "My Lord, you are showing me my former condition. Many times I didn't pay any attention to the word. Now I see why I lost all my strength. I see why I wasn't getting

any messages from you. It was because I was busy with other things and I didn't have the word in my heart. Please teach me how to engrave your word in my heart so I can love you."

"My child, pay attention to your book *Loving God* and try to remember the words in it. Teach others, but also teach yourself to hold onto the words that give you life, strength, direction, peace, and joy."

"Thank you, Lord Jesus, for direction. Let my heart be engraved with your word so I can learn about your love. I love you."

11. A Sad Woman

Jesus took the little girl to a town where many people were walking around with sad looks on their faces. No joy, smile, or cheer was visible there. The town had a dark colored building named the Grieving People's Hotel. When they walked in, the employees sitting at the front desk had such sad faces that it seemed tears could fall at any moment. Everyone she saw walking in the hallways was also sad.

The girl asked Jesus, "Why are all these people sad?"

"My loving daughter, there are many people who are going through hardships because sad things have happened to them. Many of them lost their loved ones, and the people you see are not healed. Once, you were in this place too."

The girl suddenly realized that this place was familiar. She had lost her sister and her husband to car accidents. The first time, she stayed in the hotel for many years because she didn't know how to let her sister go. When her husband died, she thought she should stay there until she died in order to honor him. The Lord convinced her not to hold on to the past and to let her husband go if she wanted to be healed from her broken heart.

"Lord Jesus, I remember—I was trying to hold onto my husband and you didn't let me because you didn't want me to live in misery."

"Many of my children are grieving. What they don't realize is that this life is temporary. The eternal life in heaven is what they need to look forward to, but they stay in this hotel instead. As long as they look back at what they have lost, they can't function. Instead, they live in misery and sadness. They can't do my work effectively when they are looking back at what they have lost. What I want you to do is to teach them how to let it go and how to look up to me. That way they can learn to live again."

"Lord Jesus, teach me how to do it."

"Keep telling them of my love. Tell them this life is temporary. Everything they have is mine and no one can claim it. Many think that they own something or someone, and that's why grief can immobilize them."

"Lord, I didn't know that grief could immobilize my heart when I lost my husband."

"My loving daughter, don't use the word 'lost.' You didn't lose anything. You didn't own your husband. Your husband is my son. He doesn't belong to anyone but me. Everything I have created is mine. People don't understand that."

"I'm sorry Lord. I'm used to using the word 'lost.' How can I express that my husband has gone to heaven?"

"This is what you can say, 'In my Father's glorious house, my husband is dancing for Jesus and praising him. I will meet him there someday if the Lord wants me to. All I have is not mine but the Lord's.'"

"Wow, Lord, you are amazing. You are the best. You answered my prayers so that I don't even miss my husband anymore. Some people couldn't believe it, but I know you answered my prayers and completely healed me from my broken heart. It was a miracle. You healed me so quickly— within three months of his passing. I couldn't believe it. If you hadn't healed me, I couldn't have followed you. I'm glad you convinced me to let my husband go."

"My loving child, I made your heart and I can heal you. You have experienced healing because you asked for it. Many don't know that I can heal them from sadness as well as from broken hearts. You knew that your grief was hindering your relationship with me. Your focus was on what you didn't have and you didn't know that I could heal you. You learned that as long as you hold on to your husband, you will live in misery. I can heal people from half-frozen hearts. I can give them a new heart that will be filled with my love."

"Lord, I want to love you and serve you more than anyone. You have become an important part of my life. You

have cured my loneliness and misery. I'm so happy with you.
I don't even feel alone because you always walk with me.
There is no feeling of loneliness when I am with you. This is
your doing—I am so thankful that you are teaching me about
your love."

"My loving daughter, that's what I am saying about your
love. A while back, I asked you what you wanted from me.
You said that you wanted to have love for me. That pleased
me. That's what you are getting, but your love for me will only
be complete when you spend time in silence before me. I
want you to kindle the fire of love in your heart with my loving
words of life. Also, you have to pray in silence in my presence
to be able to listen to the loving words from my heart. I am so
pleased with you when you come to my presence. You spend
time with me and listen to me. Some people talk to me the
whole time when they come to my presence. They have no
interest in listening to my heart and they don't know what
silent prayer does. I want you to remind them to listen so that
I can speak to them. I am looking for people who try to listen
to my voice and understand my love so they can learn to love
me."

"Jesus, help me to listen to you so I can speak for you."

"That's what I want you to do. What I share with you,
I want you to share with others so they can understand my
heart."

12. An Empty Bucket

The girl asked, "Lord, what do you think I should pray
about?"

Jesus answered, "My loving child, I am so glad that you
are asking that question. Pray that my will be done in your
life."

"Jesus, I will pray that your will be done in my life. What
is your will?"

"My will for you is that you will love me more than anyone or anything, and you will help the people that I want you to help. There are certain people I want you to help. If you use your energy to help the people that you want to help, you may not be helping the ones I want you to help."

"How can I learn your will so that I can help the people you want me to help?"

Jesus smiled. "My loving child, I want you to spend more time in silence in my presence. Listening to me in silent prayer is the key to understanding my heart."

"What else?"

"You have to let go of trying to get any approval from others. Instead, obey the Holy Spirit. Much of the time, people don't understand my will for them. Instead of encouraging you to obey me, they will try to block you and stop you from doing what I want you to do. What you need is my approval and the Holy Spirit's confirmation. Just go and do what I ask you to do instead of seeking others' approval. You will be discouraged when you try to get approval from other people. It will distract you from doing what I asked you to do. You will learn to do what I want you to do when you spend time with me in silent prayer. You have to let go of the desire to gain other people's love and approval. I will be your comfort. I will be your encouragement. I will be everything you need."

"Lord, will you teach me how to spend time with you? I have so many things to do. I have many people that I need to encourage and mentor. They want to talk to me and I am having a difficult time explaining that I need to spend time with you."

"My daughter, you won't have anything to give if you are not healed. People who have an empty bucket don't have anything to give. When you spend your time with other people more than with me, your heart will become empty. You will know when you have nothing to give. Look inside of your bucket."

The girl didn't realize that she had a bucket in her heart until now. It was completely empty. She said, "Lord, I didn't even realize that I had this bucket. Why didn't I see it before?"

"You can see your own bucket only with spiritual eyes. Those whose eyes are opened can see it and know that they have nothing to give. That's how people feel when they are burned out. You have experienced it before, haven't you?"

"Jesus, I didn't realize it, but yes, there were times I felt I had nothing to give and I couldn't complete a simple task. I didn't know why I felt that way. I felt immobilized, like I could not go on."

"Child, that's it. Your bucket was empty and you were starving. You didn't have anything left to give. If you want to know my will, you have to spend time with me. Practice silent prayer so you can hear from me. Even if you are doing a wonderful ministry in your own eyes, if it's not what I think you should be doing, I will tell you to drop it and pray in silence. Many of my workers have been discouraged and felt burned out. It turned out their buckets were empty. They knew they had nothing to give. Some, however, didn't turn to me to fill their empty buckets. Instead, they stopped serving me. They realized that they didn't have the power to change people's lives. Only I can change people's lives. What they need to do is look not into their own inadequacy but rely on me for healing and come to me for strength."

"Lord, why is it so hard to get to know your will? What you are saying is that in order for me to know your will, I need to manage my time so that I can listen to you in silence."

"My loving child, you are getting it. Burn out is a sign. I am telling them to look to me. People need to be reminded to be in my presence in silent prayer for healing and new direction. Now, I want you to follow me."

13. The Heart Bucket

Jesus said, "My loving daughter, I want you to share my heart with others. Many people seek love and approval from others, and they become disappointed and discouraged. Rightly so, I have given them an empty bucket of love and approval in their heart. It can be filled only by my love and approval. Many don't know about this and continue looking for love and approval from other people."

"Jesus, please tell me what this bucket is about."

Jesus stopped and showed her the lines inside the bucket. It was divided into four sections.

He said, "This bucket has four sections. The first section is called faith. When people open their heart to me and come to believe, they have faith in me. The first part will then be filled. The second section is called service. When people start serving others in my name, they fill it halfway. Many people, even my faithful workers, stay on the second section. This is sad, because they don't come to me to get to know my heart. They always feel empty even though they are doing many good things."

The girl asked, "Lord, this is something new to me."

"Here is more. The third section is filled by seeking and loving God through prayer and worship. Those who seek me earnestly will find me. This is what many leaders are lacking. They help people according to their own plans, with a focus on building their own reputation. They gather people for their own glory. When people don't seek my heart, they follow their own passions and desires. They can't do what I want them to do. The reason people feel that they have empty hearts is because I am letting them know that their heart buckets are empty."

"How can a person fill the rest of the bucket?"

Jesus said, "If they would only seek me, they would find a treasure, which is my heart of love. With this, they will be able to do what I want them to do. The last section is for those who truly understand my love for them. Though someone may be seeking me earnestly, there comes a time that I show myself to them. When that happens, their heart will overflow with my love for them and their love for me. When the bucket is full and overflowing, others can benefit by understanding my love and presence through them. My love for my workers is great, but until they turn to me, they can't fill their buckets. Many of my workers follow their own desires and follow the world in order to please themselves or others. I will teach you more about that bucket."

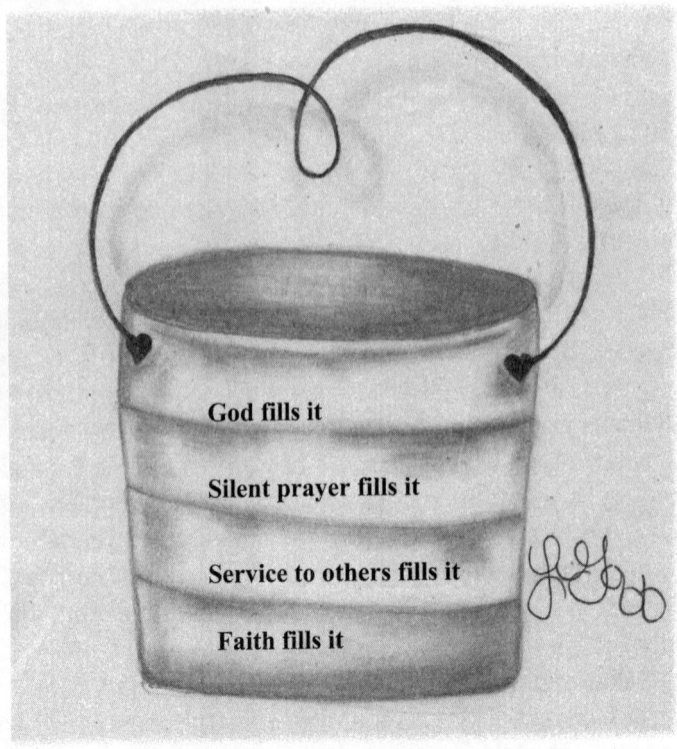

God fills it

Silent prayer fills it

Service to others fills it

Faith fills it

14. Grace

The girl was curious about her bucket. She asked, "Jesus, How full is my bucket?"

"It's about halfway full."

She was disappointed. "Is that all? That must be the reason why I felt I wanted to feel your love and approval so badly. I wanted to hear from you how special I am and how much you love me. My bucket was only half full though. That's why I felt my heart was still empty."

"My loving child, I have complete love and approval for you. In order to understand it, you have to seek me with all your heart until you find me."

"Jesus, can you tell me why I only have half of my bucket filled? I thought my bucket had more than that."

"You have faith and you are serving me, so you have filled two sections. That's where you are. The third stage is to have a close loving relationship by going into deep silence and listening to me. Many people don't realize that they will eventually run out of energy to serve me unless they go into deep silence and listen so that they can get into a loving relationship with me. You have neglected to spend time with me in personal worship and silent prayer. You say that you are busy with the ministry. However, until people are in my presence in silence they can't get to know me and hear my loving voice. You have been seeking love and approval from others through ministry."

"Lord Jesus, I am so sorry. Please forgive me. I was seeking love and approval from others. It felt good. Eventually, I needed it continuously and I didn't even realize that what I was getting from them would not fill my bucket."

"My loving daughter, your focus was on ministry, but deep inside, you sought other people's love and approval. That's where you failed. Your ministry became more important than me because you looked for love and approval in the wrong place. Your focus was not on me but on people. Actually, your focus has been on you. Now, what did you feel when they couldn't fill your empty bucket?"

"Lord, when I received love and approval from people, I felt I needed more. I kept needing more and I didn't even realize that's what I was doing. I didn't realize that what I needed was your love and approval. What people gave me was never enough for me, but instead of coming to you to fill my empty bucket, I looked for what I didn't have on my own. I kept trying to fill it without realizing how many holes it had."

Jesus smiled. "My child, recognizing that is the beginning of your healing. What people don't have, they can't give. They can't fill your empty bucket, but my love can. Do

you understand that I called you to silent prayer so I could talk to you about your spiritual condition?"

The girl looked up to Jesus with admiration. "Lord, you are the best. No one was able to tell me why I was feeling drained. People couldn't give me what I needed and I didn't have anything left to give. Now I know why my bucket is only half full. I need to work on seeking you earnestly by spending more time with you than I have been. I understand why you called me to spend time in silent prayer in order to hear from you."

Jesus looked pleased. "My daughter, that's what I wanted you to know. My grace is sufficient for you. I want you to share what I am telling you with others so that they will be able to see when their bucket is half empty. When people come to silent prayer to listen to me, they fill the third section, while I fill the last one. I will speak my loving words to my children and I will fill their empty hearts with my love and approval. When that happens, love will flow out of them. Then they will be able to understand my heart. They will know what I want them to do to help others. They will understand their calling and learn how to build up my kingdom. They will have the humble heart and wisdom to follow what I ask of them. They will have the courage to do what I ask them to do, even though it may cause hardships. They will be able to plant the seed of the gospel to help the poor and hungry ones who are dying and crying out to me. That person will be able to love me with all their heart, mind, soul, and strength and do what I want them to do."

"Wow, Lord, I want to be a person who can please you and love you. I want to have a humble heart, and the wisdom to understand your heart and your plans for my life. I want to have the courage to do what you ask me to do, and to be able to endure hardship for your sake. What should I do?"

"My loving child, the most important habit you need to develop is to worship me everyday and pray. Listen to my voice and the words that I speak to you. That will give you wisdom to share with others. You have been too focused on your ministry. What's more important, ministry or me?"

"Lord, you are more important in my life. You know that."

"My daughter, you spend your time the way that you want. What you don't understand is that you need to know what I want you to do. Those who follow me need to listen to the Holy Spirit to learn how to manage their time. The Holy Spirit has been speaking to you, telling you that you need to spend five hours a day in prayer, but you have been ignoring it. In order for you to be fed and get strength in your ministry, the more you reach out, the more you need to spend time with me to get direction. The problem you had was that you

had your own plans of how to serve me. You have no idea of how I want to use you."

"Lord, I am sorry. I was missing out on listening to you."

"That's why I called you into silent prayer, so that you could understand my plans for you."

"Thank you, Lord. You have so much compassion to wait this long for me to look to you."

"My loving child, I want you to focus on listening so you will understand my deep desires and my plans for you."

"Lord, I will. From now on, I will listen to you. I realize now how I ran out of energy because I looked for other ways to fill my empty bucket. Please forgive me."

"I forgive you my daughter. My love for you is so great. I want your bucket to be filled with my love so you can share it with others."

"Lord, I want my bucket to be filled not just 100%, but 150%, so my love for you will overflow and I don't have to look for others love and approval."

"The reason many of my workers are looking for love and approval from others is because they don't know that I am the only one who can fill their empty buckets. You need to remind them."

"Lord, why is this bucket called a bucket of love and approval? Can you explain to me what it means to get approval from you?"

"Many people who don't have respect for my word can't get my approval. Their buckets will be empty. The problem is, people put their own reasoning above my words, as well as try to get others' love and approval. This doesn't work because what they are looking for is not in other people. People's words don't have the power. Only my word has the power to break sinful and unholy thoughts. When people obey my words and pray, I will fill the bucket of love and approval. The Holy Spirit will give them peace and joy. I want you to see how people fall into sin and try to get the love and approval of others. Look at my hands. The more you understand my love, by listening to my loving words in my presence, the more your empty bucket will be filled."

The girl touched Jesus' rough hands and cried, "Thank you, Jesus, for dying for my sins. I love you and praise you for what you have done for me."

15. A Beggar's Bucket

Jesus took her to a remote town where there seemed to be many beggars. Each one carried a bucket. As the girl got closer to them, she realized that they were not beggars. All of them were wearing business suits.

They seemed to be fine, judging from their outside appearances, but she could tell that these people had been starving. All the people had empty, tired looks on their faces. Their buckets had words written on them: love and approval. Many people were trying to find others who could share their food to fill their buckets. None of them had food to share.

The girl was skipping and then asked, "Lord, you said that the bucket you give to people is in the heart, so why are these people carrying buckets in their hands?"

"My loving daughter, the buckets you see in their hands are the buckets that people gave them. Everyone is given a bucket from people when they are born. It is a bucket that measures what's important in their own culture and what's important in their own eyes. It's their way of trying to decide who can receive more love and approval from others. What they don't realize is that beggars' buckets have holes in them. They cannot truly be filled. Many people constantly try to fill the beggar's bucket but they end up hurting others in the process. They try to receive what people don't have to give. Love and approval from me will fill their heart bucket."

"Lord, I didn't realize that what I am carrying is a measuring bucket of how much others give me. When people

show love and approval, it is only temporary. I have to learn
from you how I should handle this."

"My child, throw away the beggar's bucket in your hand.
The reason you get hurt is because you expect love and
approval that people don't have. Everyone has an empty
bucket, so they can't fill yours."

The girl looked at the bucket in her hand. "Now I know
why I got hurt. I tried to fill this bucket. I received a lot of love
and approval but there is nothing in the bucket because it's
full of holes. I am going to throw it away."

She threw the bucket into the garbage. Suddenly, she felt a heavy weight lifted off of her. She started jumping high and said, "Lord, I didn't know that I was carrying a heavy burden on my shoulder. Now, I can jump high!"

Jesus smiled. "My loving child, as long as you try to get other people's love and approval, you will carry a big burden. Let go of all the expectations of how others should love you and approve of what you are doing. Then you can do what I want you to do."

"Lord, I am so thankful that you are teaching me that I don't need to beg for the love and approval of others. Let me remain in this condition until I get to my father's home."

"Many people are in bondage when they try to fill the beggar's bucket. They don't know they need to let go of it. They also forget to seek love and approval from me. They ignore their heart bucket, which only I can fill. I want you to remind them that I love them. I want to heal them. I want to have a close loving relationship with them. That's what I want to have with you."

"Lord, thank you so much for calling me to silent prayer. If you hadn't called me to pray, I wouldn't have known what I was doing wrong. I didn't even realize that I was carrying a beggar's bucket."

Jesus' face was bright. He said, "My loving daughter, I am glad that you are listening. Keep praying that each of my workers will seek me with all their heart, mind, soul, and strength. Those who seek me earnestly will find me. People who are after other people's love and approval will only get hurt because people don't have what I have—love, true love, that fills their empty heart bucket. Follow me, I have many more things to show you."

16. A Spiritual Hospital

Jesus took her to a hospital where many of his workers were being treated. One man sat on the bed sobbing.

Jesus said to her, "This man is one of my workers. He didn't spend enough time with me. He starved himself, but didn't even realize it. He was busy counting the gifts he received from others who had good intentions. This man lost interest in me, and focused on others' gifts. He had no interest in knowing my will for his life. Instead of seeking me, he sought his own interest. He took care of his material investment but not his spiritual investment. He eventually lost faith in me because he was blinded by material things. He thought he could move the mountain with money. He misunderstood. I can move mountains for him, but he relied

on his own wealth. He lost everything when others robbed and tricked him. After that, he realized he shouldn't have relied on material things. He is repenting now. He realized that what he needs is me, and nothing else."

"Lord, this is a difficult lesson for me, since I also relied on material things and got into lots of trouble. What do you think I should do to prevent these kinds of things from happening to me?"

"Seek my will for your life. My will is to teach you about my love. When you understand my love for you, your heart bucket will be filled. Then you will be fed and can share with other hungry people."

"Thank you, Jesus. Help me to understand your love so I can love you more. What could I do without you? Nothing."

"Child, you are getting the message. You may be able to do something, but it's not always fruitful if you do not follow my will and experience healing through me. Come and follow me. I will teach you about my love."

17. A Stone of Different Colors

As they walked along, Jesus took her to a beach where the rocks by the river were shining precious stones. They were more beautiful than the previous stones she had seen on earth. Then she saw a little stone which was bright and shiny on one side and black on the other. Jesus picked it up and gave it to her. The girl took the stone and turned it around, wondering what was happening.

"Jesus, what's wrong with this stone? It shines beautifully on one side but the other side looks gloomy and black..."

"My loving daughter, many of my workers follow my word half-heartedly. They depend on my word for some things, but they reject it on other issues to follow their own reasoning and fleshly desires."

"Why, Lord?"

"They think they can interpret the words as they wish. I want you to speak the truth when you teach. The truth will set people free from sin and the devil's chains. People who are not following my word are deceived by worldly standards."

"Jesus, forgive me for not truly believing in your words to know what is right and wrong. Please forgive me when I only believe a part of your words because of my rebellious heart."

"I forgive you daughter. I want you to know that there are many people who look for others' love and approval. They don't trust my word of life and they rely on their own reasoning. I want to tell you that there are many who have thrown my word in the trash and they think that what they are thinking is right. One part of the Bible that has been rejected by many is the part about homosexuality. I want you to warn

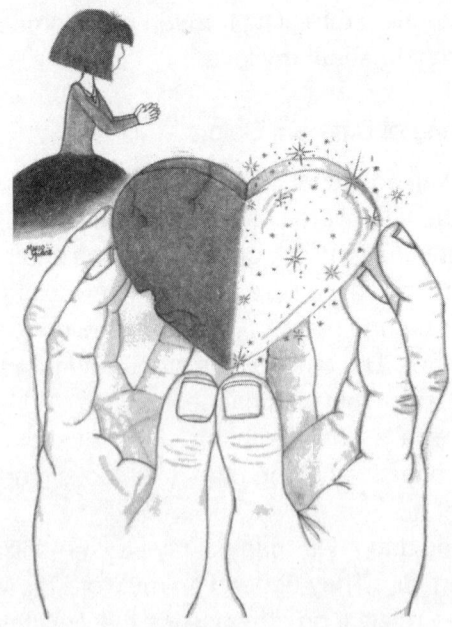

them that they are not following my words but their own fleshly desires."

"I thought that you love sinners and you do not condemn anyone? I believe your word is truth, but I am upset with those who point at homosexuals, yet fail to see their own sins. Why are you pointing them out when there are many other sins?"

"My loving child, I don't condemn anyone. I love everyone. I didn't come to the world to condemn it but to save it. Many are deceived by the devil and think I am against them. I am not against them. All that I want for them to do is obey my word without trying to justify their sins. Many are under the devil's attack and they are hurting. The devil has deceived many. They think I don't care about them, but I do. I died to save them from eternal hell."

"Lord Jesus, thank you for dying on the cross for my sins so I could be saved."

"My loving daughter, I am glad that you recognize it. Many don't focus on what I did to save them. They think I condemn them. Why would I condemn them? I want them to turn to me and understand my love. If anyone falls into sin, all they have to do is repent. I clean their clothes so they can shine white as snow. All they need to do is believe in my word and my love, and they will find rest for their souls. The problem is, when people fall into sin, they think I condemn them. Instead of coming to me, they leave me. Therefore, many wander around in the bushes where the wolves can catch them. Many people are in the wilderness where the

scorpions and snakes roam. They don't know where to turn for help. I want my lost sheep to be found so that I can heal them with my love."

"Lord, I pray that you will help those who are not willing to obey you."

"My loving daughter, keep praying that my sheep will be found. If you can save one lost sheep, there will be joy in heaven."

"Lord, please forgive me for ignoring your words. I have put my own reasoning above your word from time to time. Please bless me with the wisdom to understand your word. Help me to delight in your word so I can teach others what you want me to teach them. Have mercy on us when we are lost in the wilderness with our own reasoning."

"My loving child, come and follow me. I have many things to teach you."

18. A Leaking Roof

Jesus took her to a town that had many houses that were damaged due to heavy rain. The girl went into her house and learned that the roof had a leak. It was not just one leak, but many leaks, and it ruined many things. She tried with all her might to get the water out of the rooms but she felt helpless.

She asked, "What happened to my house, Lord? It has many leaks in the roof."

He replied, "My daughter, the spiritual condition of many of my workers is like that. Their roofs leak in many places. They need to make changes. Many are not truly loving me. They serve me half-heartedly, so their houses leak. They feel helpless because there are too many holes. They have waited too long to fix the problem. They relied on themselves instead of me. They didn't come to me to talk about how to fix the roof before the rains came. They could have prevented

this if they had come to me and asked for help. Many problems in life can be solved when my guidance is sought."

"Lord, why do I have problems like this?"

"Until people realize my importance and seek me earnestly, their roofs will have holes that ruin their houses. What good is it to gain the whole world yet lose your soul? My word is the foundation of your faith. Prayer will build the beams and the rest."

"Forgive me for not praying enough. Help me to fix my roof. What do I need to do? I feel so overwhelmed."

"It's prayer, my daughter. Prayer will fix the leaking roof. What you are seeing is your spiritual condition."

"Thank you, Lord. I will pray more so that my house will be fixed."

19. Cleaning People

Jesus took her to a town where everything looked perfect and clean. The girl was enjoying the sun and the flowers next to the sidewalk. Then Jesus took her to a building where many ladies were putting their brooms into a closet.

Jesus said, "These are my workers. They pray day and night. They are the ones who make the roads clean for others to enjoy them."

"Lord Jesus, this is the most clean and beautiful town I have ever visited. I was surprised to see how spotless the roads were when we first entered this town."

"These women pray day and night to help others to clean their hearts. The road and the town symbolize a person's heart. A person who prays and spends time with me has the power to help others who are in need. I have answered many people's prayers when they cried out for help."

"Lord Jesus, I am really sorry that I neglect praying for others. Now I realize that others did all the hard work of praying for me."

"My daughter, there are many who are praying for you because you are working for me. I also want you to pray for others who are working for me. Many of my workers are dying and they are in need of healing. What they don't realize is that they need to come to me for healing. Pray that they will seek me earnestly, so they can find me and experience healing."

"Lord, I am learning that even though I thought I was doing well, it was because someone else was praying for me. I didn't know that. Please forgive me."

"Many of my workers are dying from lack of prayer. I don't want you to fall into that trap."

"Help me to hold on to you. I want to keep walking with you so that I can hear your voice and experience healing."

"Tell others the importance of praying for each other. Tell them to find me through prayer."

"Thank you, Lord, for helping me to realize that I need to pray for others."

20. A Man's Feast

Jesus took her to a town where there were many homeless and hungry people on the streets. Some lived

under a bridge. There were many children and some were sleeping in a box. A mother was holding a baby in a ragged blanket, and that was all she had. There seemed to be no end to this line of homeless people.

The girl said, "Lord, why are there so many homeless and hungry people on the street, especially children?"

"Many are going through much suffering and my workers need to take care of them. Come, I will show you something else."

By the end of the bridge, suddenly there stood many big houses. Jesus took the girl to a mansion where a man had a feast all to himself. The table was full of food and this man was so huge that he had a hard time getting up, but he kept eating.

Jesus said, "My daughter, you are seeing people's spiritual conditions. Many of my workers are still eating though they are already full. They are rich, but don't know how to share their food with others who are starving in the

world. The homeless and hungry on the street are in need of their help. My workers need to get out of the church and start sharing my loving word with the hungry people. They need to plant the seed of hope. Sadly, many of my children don't know how to share what I have given them. Those who have received a lot are expected to share what I have given them."

The girl cried, "I am so sorry, Jesus. I have been feeding myself and I thought it was good enough for me. I didn't think about telling others about Christ. I didn't know that they were starving and dying. Please help me so that I will be able to share."

Jesus smiled. "My loving daughter, those who can feed others will also be healthy. Just feeding yourself will only make you lazy. Let others know that I am concerned about those who study the Bible without sharing it with the starving people on the street. There are many who do not come to church because they don't feel they have clean clothes, but they need me to help them clean up. They need my word to cure them from hopelessness. My word can raise the dead. My daughter, tell others to share what they have. When I give to people, I don't just give it to them to keep it for themselves, but to share it with others. Those who receive a lot are required to share a lot."

The girl felt shame. "Lord, I am not sure if other people can understand what I am trying to say. I used to think that Bible study was just for me. I didn't know that I had to share."

"My loving child, everything I give is meant to be shared. When you don't share, you can't grow. See why my people don't have joy? They only feed themselves. To find joy, you need to give what you have received."

"Lord, I think I do remember a time when someone appreciated that I read the Scriptures to them. That touched me and made me happy."

"That's it. Share what you have learned. If people don't share, they are hiding what they have received. I don't want you to hide what you have learned from me. What I tell you, tell others."

The girl said, "Oh Lord, help me to have the courage to share what you are telling me. Many times I worry about what other people think because people misunderstand me."

"My loving daughter, that's because they don't know my relationship with you. I have called you to train the leaders so they can feed hungry souls. Many people in prison are feeling hopeless, but you can plant the seed of hope with my word. I want to remind the leaders to look to me and develop a close relationship with me. I want spiritual leaders to pay attention to my call. Many keep following their own wisdom and fall into the trap of the devil's tricks. Many get captured by sinful desires and are ineffective in ministry."

The girl was crying, "Lord, how can you call on a little girl like me and ask her to tell others? They won't listen to me."

Jesus looked at her and said gently. "My daughter, it doesn't matter who listens to you. What's important is for you to be obedient. I will put you in a place where your voice will be heard. I will help you spread the books that you are writing to places you can't even imagine. I will give you a crown of flowers, then others will know that you are walking with me. I want you to be courageous. I will give you strength. Remember, you cannot follow me if you can't carry your cross. You have to die to the world to be able to follow me. You have to let go of what others think about you and focus instead on loving me, then the rest will be easy for you to obey. If you love me, you will do what I ask you to do."

The girl sat on the grass. She wiped her tears and said, "Lord, it's hard for me to obey and follow you. You are asking me to warn others to repent and change their ways. You want them to follow you, no matter what the cost. Is there anything I can teach them?"

Jesus looked at her with a big smile. "Yes, I want you to teach them that I love them. The message you are to give them is that I love them. When people learn from me, their lives will be changed and their wounds will be healed. Their empty hearts will be filled with my love and my peace."

"Thank you, Lord. Let me tell the world of your love." The girl started dancing in the grass and Jesus started dancing with her.

The girl said, "Lord Jesus, fill my heart with your love. Fill my heart with love for you. Fill the world with your love. Fill people's hearts with love for you. Let my love grow like a rose in your garden. Let me plant the seed of your love in the wilderness, even among thorn bushes, so they may see your loving flower take over everywhere. Let me see miracles in my ministry. Let your seed of love spread throughout the world so the hungry children will be fed, the sick will be healed, and the dead souls will be raised by your loving words. Let the hopeless find hope. Let your love heal the wounded people. Let me love you, Lord Jesus. Fill my empty bucket with your love. Let my heart be filled with your loving words of life."

Jesus said, "My daughter, it's time to go out and look for the sheep lost in the bushes before the wolves can find them."

The girl followed Jesus, skipping. Walking with Jesus was the most glorious journey she could ever have imagined. She was glad that she had decided to follow him.

21. Ice Fishing

Jesus took the girl to a frozen pond. He made a little hole, dropped a fishing line into it, and sat there waiting.

The girl asked, "Lord, it's cold out here. What are you trying to teach me?"

Jesus didn't say anything. He just kept waiting. She was getting impatient and said, "What are you trying to teach me, Lord?"

Jesus turned to her and said, "My daughter, many of my workers are not listening to me, so they are not catching anything. I understand their agony. I am feeling their disappointment. Do you understand what I am trying to tell you now? I try to tell my disciples where to catch fish, but they are not listening. There are many hungry people on the road and many feel that no one cares for them. You need to find these lost sheep. My lost sheep are crying out in pain, but many of my workers don't hear them. There are many who can't come to church because they feel unworthy. They feel unwelcome. They feel that church is only for rich people. I want you to reach out to those who feel unloved and undervalued, to let them know that they won't feel unwelcome in the church."

The girl cried, "Lord, please forgive me. I always wanted comfort and I wanted to be loved, but I looked for that from other people. My heart bucket was empty and I wasn't able to provide others with love and comfort. Please help those who are feeding these hungry people."

Jesus said, "I have many who are working for the people on the streets but I need more. There are many who feel they are not worthy of receiving my love. I love them, but I need someone to go out and tell them."

"Lord, I am sorry that I wasn't reaching out to the people who desperately need you. Please forgive me for not praying for the leaders who are reaching out to these people."

Jesus got up and said, "I want you to reach out to the leaders and tell them what I want them to do. There are too many lost sheep wandering around the streets and they feel lonely. They need my love and care. I need people to go out and bring the lost sheep to my house. Many of my workers are fishing in places where there are no fish. They are discouraged because they don't see results. What they don't realize is that the lost sheep are not where they are looking. They need to go out to the streets to find the people who feel they can't come to my house."

"Lord, help me to do what you want me to do."

"My daughter, I want you to spend time in prayer. Then you will throw your net to the places I want you to be. In this way, you can catch people for my kingdom. They will follow me. When you try to catch fish and you can't, you need to go somewhere else to fish."

"Jesus, please guide my path so that I will be able to help the lost sheep. Help me to help many leaders so they can also find lost sheep and bring them to your house."

"My daughter, the time is coming that there will be a great harvest. This last harvest has to be in the place where people are hurting and searching for me. I want you to continue to listen. Pray that you will be guided by the Holy Spirit to reach out to them. If you don't listen, you will miss the opportunity to be a part of the harvest team. Your silent prayer is the key. Shut the other voices out and listen only to me."

"My Lord Jesus, help me to pray in silence and to listen to you."

"My loving daughter, time is short. Many don't realize that their ministry time is very short on earth, especially those who don't listen to the Holy Spirit. Many are wasting time doing things that I didn't ask them to do. They end up following their own sinful desires. Blessed are those who are coming to my presence, listening, and obeying."

"Lord, help me to do what you want me to do."

"My child, I also want you to remind people to pray more for the leaders who are in need of faith, wisdom, strength, and courage. Many who don't have these things fall away from the tasks I have given them. I don't want them to miss this harvest, but it's easy to miss. Many have the opportunities but don't see them."

"Please help me not to miss out on the opportunity to be part of the great harvest team in the last days."

Jesus was smiling. "As long as you continue to listen and obey, you will be a part of this team. Come, I have more to teach you. I love you daughter. I want you to follow me."

The girl followed Jesus and started singing, "Lord Jesus, thank you for your love and your loving voice. Thank you for sharing your heart. Help me to remember to pray to listen to you. Help me to hear a clear message from you. I want to be a part of this harvest. Open my heart to understand where the lost sheep are and how I can help those in need of your care. I praise you, Lord Jesus, for your compassion. Let me know your compassion and love. Let me have the Holy Spirit's anointing to do what I need to do. Let me bring a smile to your face with my love and obedience."

The girl danced as they walked along. Jesus looked pleased and smiled at her. Soon, Jesus started skipping and dancing with her. The sun was coming up and it started melting the icy road. The warm feeling of sunshine melted her heart just like Jesus' love.

22. A Wounded Man

The girl went on a journey with many others who seemed to be in God's family. A leader of the group started arguing with a young man. Suddenly, the leader attacked the young man. It happened so fast that no one could stop them.

The girl was in a panic. The leader ended up on the floor motionless. The young man had been much stronger than the leader. The young man left and the girl thought that the leader was dead. She didn't know what to do. When she tried to find people to help care for him, there was no one around. All the other people had disappeared. The girl touched the leader's face to check if he was breathing. She felt a little warmth on his check and was relieved that he was still alive.

The leader soon got up and said, "That was a big blow. I feel like my arm's been cut off."

The girl was sad. Why can't family get along and help each other instead of fighting? Even though there was an argument, the leader had made a mistake by attacking the young man. Violence is not what she wanted to see. She was disappointed.

Then, she remembered Jesus and turned to him. "Jesus, what happened here? This leader was helping the young man, but then they fought like enemies. I am not even sure whom I can talk to. There were many people with us when we started this journey, but now I don't see anyone. They all disappeared because of this fight. No one was left to stop them."

Jesus looked sad. "My daughter, what you saw was a spiritual fight. Many of my workers don't know how to solve problems. They don't come to me and ask me for any advice. They choose to fight the spiritual battle with their own wisdom, which leads to failure every time. Instead of coming to me for wisdom on how to fight the battle, these people fight with their own strength. That's what the devil wants. When people fall into sin and don't forgive others, they end up falling into a trap of violence. The devil is able to get a hold on them. When that happens, my workers focus only on solving problems, to the point that they forget about what they are called to do. That's what the devil wants. Until my children can repent their sins and turn to me, they are in a prison of anger and fear."

"Lord, I remember I was not kind and gentle to people when they mistreated me. Please forgive me for my lack of prayer. I didn't ask for your wisdom, rather I made the mistake of carrying out violent thoughts and actions. I knew you weren't happy when you told me to ask others for forgiveness. Please help me so that I can learn to solve problems peacefully with your wisdom and love."

"My daughter, I forgive you. Many of my workers don't learn how to be humble before me and they don't ask for advice. When they learn how to be humble, to pray, and to spend time with me, then they will see the big picture of what's happening. Then they can solve problems peacefully. I hate violence. It creates a spiritual prison for the victims as well as those who commit the violent acts. Many of my workers don't know this so they think, say, and act however they want. They don't understand that the mistreatment of others will hinder their relationship with me. What I am looking for is a person who can free others from a spiritual prison of anger and violence. When my workers learn how to be kind and gentle, they will be able to teach others."

"Lord, why is it so hard to learn this lesson of kindness and love? We all need to love others as we love ourselves. Why are there so many wars where people think it is alright to not only hurt others, but kill them as well?"

"My daughter, I want you to know that there are many people who think about greed and power. There are many who don't promote me and my kingdom. Instead, they promote themselves. Those who practice violence and hurt others will be judged. They need to know that. People need to come to me to learn how to plant the seed of peace."

"My Lord, how can we create peace?"

"Preach the gospel. When people are touched by my love and wisdom, they will take care of others instead of promoting their own selfish gain. Love creates peace."

"Lord, I want to create peace."

"I want you to keep following me and learning about my love. Teach others that I love them. You have been doing this, but I will help you do even more with your books. Reach out to the poorest people—those who can't buy the books or hear the gospel. Many of my workers are trying to save people who can't be saved unless others reach out to them. I want you to encourage my workers who are doing this already. I want you to reach out to the leaders and share this message with them."

"Lord, guide me to do what you want. I pray that the poorest people will come to know you, understand your love, and learn to love you. I pray that your workers, who are sacrificing their lives to preach the gospel in the jungle, will be protected by angels. I pray that the people who commit violent acts towards others will be convicted by the Holy Spirit

and come to know that they have to change their ways. I pray for the victims of violence, that they will be freed from the prisons of anger and fear. Lord, help me to free others from the spiritual prisons of greed and selfishness. I pray for everyone who is in bondage to sin and violence. Help me to create peace, Lord."

Jesus smiled at her and said, "Keep praying and continuing to help others in need of spiritual direction and healing. Fight the good fight, my daughter."

"Help me to fight the good fight and achieve victory, Lord."

"My loving daughter, I have already achieved victory. All you have to do is walk with me with a clean heart and proclaim it."

"Thank you, Lord Jesus, for reminding me of that."

"Now, follow me. I want to show you what I have in mind."

The girl followed Jesus. She sang. "Lord Jesus, you have achieved victory. You did this for everyone. Help me to walk with you so I can proclaim victory in your name."

The girl smiled at Jesus, then they started dancing and singing with the birds.

23. Clothesline

Jesus took the girl to a place where there was a pair of pants on a clothesline. She felt a gentle breeze, which made the pants move with the wind.

"Lord, what are you trying to tell me?"

"My daughter, when you decided to give me your plans for the future I started cleaning your heart."

"Why did you clean my heart when I gave you my future plans?"

"Because when you try to do things your way, you end up following your own desires instead of mine. When you do

156

that, you can't pay attention to my plans. This is a problem that affects many of my workers. They already made up their minds how they think they should serve me, and I am unable to share my plans with them. They are interested in their own plans, not mine."

"Jesus, you showed me my condition. At first, I didn't want your plan for my life at all. That's why I didn't want to go into the ministry. After you helped me to make the decision to follow you, I still tried to have my own plans. Now, I realize how much I have been ignoring your voice. It's because I wanted to do it my own way. Please forgive me."

"I forgive you daughter."

24. A Feast

The next place Jesus led her was a town where a big party was happening. "My loving daughter, I have invited you to attend a feast I prepared for you. Come, eat with me."

There was a big table and she began eating many delicious foods. Jesus looked at her with love in his eyes. He smiled and said, "My loving child, are you feeling better since you started eating in my presence?"

"Yes, Lord! I didn't know how hungry I was. These foods are so delicious. You sure know how to make me happy! All the foods you have prepared for me are delicious."

"My child, silent prayer is what people need in order to eat at my feast. Tell others how I fed you."

"Lord, I feel much better since you called me to silent prayer. I was dying, but now I am gaining spiritual strength."

"Whenever you come to my presence, you are filled with good food that nourishes you. Tell others how you gained strength, then they can come to my party to eat in my presence as well."

"Lord, thank you for calling me to pray in silence. Now, I feel like I can't find strength any other way. People can't feed me. Their love and approval always came with expectations. It was not unconditional."

"My loving daughter, you are finally seeing the big picture. I told you not to have anyone in your life that you talk to more than me. I don't want you to have anyone that is closer to you than me. They will all drain your energy because you can't give them what they want. You need to direct them to seek me earnestly. They can find me in silent prayer. Then, they can come to my table and eat with me. Those who pay attention to the Holy Spirit will come to silent prayer. That way I can feed them and they will gain strength. Those who are waiting to hear from me will hear my voice. I want you to teach others about this. I will put you in a high place that allows you to speak to many about this. You have already started doing it with your book project."

"Lord, I need you badly. I need to see you every moment. Listening in silence doesn't seem so hard anymore. You can speak to me when I need to hear from you."

"My loving child, I want you to take care of yourself so that you are able to take care of others."

"I am getting it, Lord. I can't do anything without you."

"You can do things, but you will not be effective if you try them on your own. Follow me, my beloved daughter. It's time to go and find the lost sheep."

Jesus was skipping and dancing, leading the way, and the girl tried to imitate him. The sun was high and the birds were singing. The girl felt loved because Jesus was with her. He held her hand. She knew that wherever Jesus led her it would be a place where he taught her lessons about his love and power. She knew she had everything that she needed.

25. Mother's Baggage

Jesus took her to a town where many people were carrying luggage. The girl's mother used to carry lots of luggage. The girl had a lot of baggage that her mother had left her. Her mother had become very sick and unable to walk. Her son tried to assist her, but it seemed like she was so weak that she wasn't able to move.

When the girl looked at the luggage, it suddenly seemed to grow tall and formidable in front of her, like a mountain range. She felt stressed because she didn't see how she could carry all of it. She turned to Jesus, "Jesus, I need your help. I can't walk with you if I have to carry all of this."

"My daughter, now is the time to pray. You will be able to move mountains with my power. You can't do it on your own. Ask others to help you. In fact, one of your tasks is to encourage others to pray more. That way they will be able to move mountains as well as help others."

"Lord, what does all this luggage contain?"

"Burdens your mother carried," Jesus replied. "She used to move many mountains through her prayers, but she can't anymore. Actually, this baggage is the burdens she carried for you for all these years. My workers need prayers. That's what she did. Now, she is not able to because she isn't well and is having a difficult time concentrating on prayers. She has done her share of prayers for you and many others. It's your turn to pray for the power to move the mountains. Pray for other leaders. Encourage others to pray for the spiritual leaders. That way they can walk with me and do what I want them to do."

"Lord, is that why I felt so weak recently? My mother hasn't been able to pray for me?"

"Yes. All these years, you were ministering with the strength of her prayers. She is unable to pray like she used to, so you need to pray more. That way you can gain strength. Now, she needs your prayers."

"Jesus, I'm sorry that I neglected praying for my mother and other spiritual leaders. Please help me to help others. How can I carry this baggage? This is too high for me to climb."

"My loving daughter, the Holy Spirit will help you pray. You will be able to move mountains. You will see. The Holy Spirit will help you by sending others to help."

"You are going to send others to help me?"

"Yes, I will, because that was your mother's prayer—that I send many people to help you. I will answer her prayers."

The girl felt grateful for her mother, who prayed for her ministry all these years. She had been able to do lots of work because of those prayers. It was her mother who, through prayers, had helped her more than she could think or imagine. The girl was in tears when she thought about her mother, who diligently prayed for her family and her ministry.

"Lord Jesus, thank you for giving me a mother who prayed for me. Since she can't pray like she used to, let me take over for her. Help me pray for my family and for others. Please help me. I can't do it on my own."

"My loving daughter, you are finally beginning to understand my heart and my plans for you. Your mother will be rewarded for her love for me and her faithfulness. She has been the crown of your head."

"Lord, I don't understand."

"That means, she is the one who put a crown on your head by praying for you. All of your many ministry opportunities were answers to her prayers."

"Thank you, Jesus, for helping me understand how my mother's prayers helped me. I see now the importance of

161

praying for others, especially your leaders, who are in desperate need of prayers to help them work for you. I need your help to carry this burden."

"My loving daughter, your burden will be light because you asked me to help you with your problem. I will teach you how to be humble. Through prayer, you can give all your burdens to me. Keep praying so I can take all your burdens away."

"Thank you, Lord, for understanding my burdens. Thank you so much for teaching me about why I needed to be healed and about my lack of prayers. Lord, help my mother and others who are hurting physically, emotionally, mentally, and spiritually. Help them to be strong. Help those who are hungry, hurting, abused, and incarcerated. Lord, send the angels to help those who are hurting all over the world. We can't do it on our own. We need your help. I need people to pray with me. Help me, Lord, to come to you in silent prayer to listen to your heart and understand your love. I love you."

The girl started dancing and suddenly all the baggage disappeared. She was overjoyed. She jumped up and down and said, "Lord, my luggage is all gone."

"Keep praying, my daughter. That's the only way you can be free from the burden. The Holy Spirit has started bringing people to help you be more effective in your ministry. They will be praying with you and will move the mountains of baggage with the power of the Holy Spirit."

"Thank you, Lord Jesus, for sending people to help me and pray with me. Together we can carry these burdens."

"Now, my daughter, it's time to go and find the lost sheep in the bushes. I will go with you and help you find them. Come and follow me."

The girl started following Jesus and singing for him. "Lord, your love and power is greater than anyone I have ever met. I know you will help me find the lost sheep."

The forest was filled with birds and the girl sang with them. Jesus looked happier than ever.

26. Cold Winter

Jesus and the girl were walking in silence. As they walked, snow started falling and they saw mountains ahead. As they traveled through the forest, the snow came down heavily, making it hard to see the road. She saw a man walking fast who said, "A Rescue Team is coming. It's dangerous around here. It's very cold." Then the man disappeared.

The girl saw a yellow helmet on the ground. Then she noticed her little sister lying on the ground nearby. She ran to her sister and picked her up. Her body was stiff and frozen, and she wasn't breathing. In a panic, the girl started shaking her sister's body to wake her up. The little girl started responding slowly, then she started breathing weakly. The girl watched as a team of people came to rescue people from the mountain. The girl put her little sister into one of the rescuer's big square slides. By then, she seemed to be completely revived. She got out of the slide and gave her big sister a tight hug. The little girl then went back to the slide.

The girl then opened her eyes and, realizing it was a vision, asked Jesus what it meant.

"My loving daughter, you were like that girl. You were dying in the cold without my love. People without me are freezing to death. My love can bring warmth and give them life. My love and healing power can be felt when people come to me in prayer. You were in the cold too long without relying on my love to give you life through prayer."

"Oh, so the little girl I saw was myself. Without you, my life has no meaning."

"My child, I give life to people. That's why they need to hear the message of love. Preach the gospel. Don't waste your time on anything else. People need to hear my message of love. They need to know that I love them. Your job is to go where I send you and speak what I want you to speak. Don't worry, I will give you the words."

"Lord, how can I teach others about your love?"

"My loving daughter, you started doing it after I called you to silent prayer. Pray that more people will hear my message of love. Don't be distracted by others, because then you will forget what I want you to do. Come and follow me. Pray that my Father will send more workers to the fields to talk about my love. The harvest is plentiful but the workers are few. I need my workers united to work for my kingdom. I want you to listen and share what I give you. Don't pay any attention to those who don't listen to my word of life. Pay attention to the Holy Spirit's directions. Then, you can do what I want you to do."

"Lord Jesus, let me hear your loving voice all the time. Let me have the courage to speak for you. Let me speak in love. I want to live to please you without worrying about what others think. I give you all the glory. Raise up the workers. Let me work with those who are obeying you. Use me fully in your service. Help me walk with you and listen to you in silence. Thank you, Jesus, for calling me to silent prayer and giving me life."

The girl was dancing and singing for Jesus. Jesus looked pleased.

"My loving child, let's look for lost sheep. They are crying out to me. I want to heal them and protect them."

"My Lord, you are more beautiful than anyone I have ever met. Your love is greater than anything I have experienced. Your love melted my heart and gave me life. Let me understand your love more so I can love you more. I love you more than anyone and anything. Let my love grow in your garden of love and beauty."

The girl sang and Jesus smiled at her.

164

27. Valley of Flowers

After they passed the snowy mountain, Jesus took her to another valley covered with dandelions. The girl was surprised to see the flowers and she started running to the beautiful yellow valley.

"Jesus, this place looks familiar. Are we in the same valley that I saw before?"

"My loving daughter, we are in the same place, but at a different time. I want you to enjoy seeing the revival. Let's have lunch here so you can enjoy it while we rest."

Jesus sat on the grass and gave the girl food and drink. As soon as she finished eating, the girl ran to the field. She started blowing the dandelion seeds into the air.

"Thank you, Jesus. You knew I missed this beautiful place. Thank you for bringing me back here, but please don't let me forget about you anymore, even when I enjoy the flowers. Let me pray silently to invite you into my everyday life. Don't let me forget that I need to talk to you and listen to you. If you want to take me to other places, help me to follow you with joy and a obedient heart."

The girl started talking to the flowers, telling them how much God loves them. The sun was high and the white clouds and blue sky revealed God's beauty. It was a perfect place with Jesus there watching her. She knew that wherever Jesus led her, it would be a happy place, but she never expected that he would take her back to the valley of beautiful dandelions where she had previously seen a revival.

"Jesus, thank you for your love. I love you."

The girl blew the seeds and sang softly. "Jesus, I love you. You are the most important person in my life. Thank you for taking me on this journey. Let my love grow like a flower and make you smile."

"I love you, daughter," he said to her with a smile.

"Jesus, what shall I tell the flowers?"

"Tell them I love them. No matter what they have done, if they repent and come to me, I will forgive them. I won't remember their sins. Tell them that I cry when they hurt. I feel their pain too. Tell them I am waiting for them to come to me. Tell them I have the power to heal their broken hearts and give them hope."

"Thank you, Lord Jesus, for the message of your love and power. Bless me with the courage to tell the world about your great love and power. I feel like I am in heaven."

"My loving child, you are. When you spend time with me, you taste a little glimpse of heaven."

"Thank you, Lord. I want others to feel the joy, peace, and happiness that I am feeling now because I am with you."

"My daughter, that's what silent prayer does. When people come to my presence and listen, they will understand my love. They need to listen to understand my heart."

"Thank you for calling me to silent prayer. If you hadn't called me for silent prayer, I wouldn't have learned what you have taught me through it. Do you still want me to continue praying silently?"

"My loving child, your silent prayer has not ended yet. In fact, you have just gotten started. You have to focus on silent prayer until you get to our heavenly Father's home. I want you to practice listening to my heart everyday. Talk to people less and talk to me more. That's the only way you can continue to understand my love for you. This goes for others as well. When they shut out outside noises and listen to my heart, they will be healed from their aches and pains. Many are too busy seeking love and approval from others and they have forgotten about me."

"Lord, help me spend more time in silence with you."

"You are finally learning how, daughter." Jesus smiled at her as she picked out some flowers. She gave them to Jesus and started singing for him. Jesus looked more pleased than ever.

"Lord Jesus, you are the most beautiful person in this valley and the world! Let me proclaim your love to all the earth. Let me understand your heart so that I can have your love. Let me understand your plans for me so I can follow you willingly. Lord, I love you, even more today than yesterday."

Jesus said, "My loving daughter, keep looking for lost sheep. I will help you to see a great revival—much more than what you have already seen. All you have to do is keep up with your silent prayers and walk with me."

The girl and Jesus started dancing. Beautiful butterflies rose up and started dancing with them. There was quiet gentleness in that valley. The love Jesus had for her was so great and the girl knew it. Jesus' love changes the world. His love changed her life and helped her give hope and direction to others. Only Jesus' love can bring life to a person and fill the empty bucket of the heart. She was grateful that the Lord taught her that lesson. She doesn't know where the Lord will lead her, but she does know that as long as he is with her, she is loved and cared for. He will show her whom she should help.

"'Get yourself ready! Stand up and say to them whatever I command you. Do not be terrified by them, or I will terrify you before them. Today I have made you a fortified city, an iron pillar and a bronze wall to stand against the whole land —against the kings of Judah, its officials, its priests and the people of the land. They will fight against you but will not overcome you, for I am with you and will rescue you,' declares the LORD." (Jeremiah 1:17-19)

Part Two:
How I Practice Silent Prayer

It took a while for me to learn that prayer is not a one way conversation. The Lord wants to speak to us. Silent prayer helps us to understand His heart and to develop a close relationship with Him.

When I am in silent prayer, I limit my conversations with other people. The Lord doesn't want me to spend as much time with other people. He would rather I spend that time listening to Him.

I don't watch TV. In fact, I don't even own a TV because it distracts me from my walk with God. I love to listen to inspirational music, but after He called me to silent prayer, He wouldn't let me listen to any music, even while driving. I have to be in silence.

I used to use music in the background during prayer, but I don't even do that anymore. Using music is meditative and can be a good tool sometimes, but I learned that it distracts me when I am in silent prayer.

I read the newspaper to know what's happening in the world, and I limit conversations. I communicate often through email, but I only use the phone if it is absolutely necessary. I don't even mentor on the phone. I focus on three disciplines: 1. Be silent and listen to God. 2. Minister to others. 3. Write books as He leads me.

The following is a simple daily silent prayer practice I developed.

(1) Dream journal: When I wake up, I write down the dreams I can remember and ask the Lord to make their

meaning clear to me. Most of the time the Lord gives me an understanding of the dreams and tells me what He wants me to know.

(2) Read and meditate on the Scripture:

I read the devotionals from the book *Loving God, 100 Daily Meditations and Prayers.*

(3) Sing for Jesus: I ask the Lord what song He would like to hear. When He doesn't respond, I sing any song that might please Him.

(4) Talk to God in prayer: I spend time praying for myself and others.

(5) Practice silent prayer: I wait in silence and say, "Lord, is there anything you want to speak to me about? Is there anything that I need to know?"

(6) Journal: If the Lord gives me words in my mind or gives me a spiritual vision, I write it down and ask Him questions to clarify my understanding. I try to pray constantly throughout the day. I also listen for his voice as I walk around.

I follow the above format before I go to sleep as well, except I don't do the dream journal. This simple practice has helped me listen to God's voice. At first I had a difficult time quieting my mind, but now it seems much easier to silence my thoughts. Silent prayer has helped me to understand God's love, His heart, and His plans for me. This gives me peace, although at times I have a difficult time obeying the Lord. I need more time in silent prayer to learn how to be obedient.

I thank God that He called me to silent prayer. If He hadn't, I couldn't have written this book to help others recognize the importance of silent prayer and taking the time to listen to God.

Part Three:
How to Practice Silent Prayer
A 30 Day Prayer Project

How to Practice Silent Prayer
A 30 Day Prayer Project

For the following 30 days, develop a habit of communicating with Jesus. Spend most of your time listening to Him. Many people listen to more than five different radio channels at a time in their mind. To hear God's voice, you need to learn to quiet your mind and listen in a state of silence.

God doesn't speak to us all the time, so be patient. The more time you spend in the Bible and in prayer, the more you will recognize His voice. Try to understand His heart. Here are some guidelines on how you can practice silent prayer.

(1) If you can, talk less with other people and shut down any outside noises. Don't watch TV or listen to music. Instead, focus on listening to God in silence throughout the day as much as possible. It's hard to quiet your mind at first, but as time goes by it gets easier. You don't always have to sit down in order to quiet your mind. You can practice silence in your mind while you walk around.

(2) Scripture reading: Pick out any gospel and read it to understand Jesus' heart. There are two ways to practice this. One way is to read any gospel for 30 minutes each day. (The Gospels are: Matthew, Mark, Luke, and John). The second is to read from one gospel a day for the next 30 days: 1) Matthew has 28 chapters; 2) Mark has 16 chapters; 3) Luke has 24 chapters; 4) John has 21 chapters. Make a chart on how you progress with this reading every day.

Prayer: "Holy Spirit, bless me with wisdom, knowledge, and revelation to understand the Scripture, Jesus' heart, and His love for me."

(3) Write down your conversations with the Lord: After reading the gospel to learn about Jesus, write a letter from Jesus stating whatever he may be speaking to your heart.

Prayer: "Lord Jesus, please speak to me and teach me everything you want me to learn from the Scriptures I read. Holy Spirit, help me to understand God's love for me and help me to have love for Him."

(4) Pray for 30 minutes each day: Talk to God for 15 minutes and listen to His voice in silence for 15 minutes. Find a quiet time to do this, but try to practice silence as much as possible throughout the day so that you can listen to God's heart.

(5) Worship God: We are created to love and worship Jesus. Paul wrote, "He is the image of the invisible God, the firstborn over all creation. For by him all things were created: things in heaven and on earth, visible and invisible, whether thrones or powers or rulers or authorities, all things were created by him and for him." (Colossians 1:15-19)

Attend worship services and worship Jesus throughout each day. Loving God is recognizing His presence. You can offer your love through praise and worship as well by giving thanks to Him.

(6) Clean your spiritual house by repenting: We can't see ourselves clearly until the Holy Spirit convicts us of our sins. Ask Him to help you.

Prayer: "Holy Spirit, if there is any sin that I need to repent, please help me to see it and ask for forgiveness."

(7) Meditation: Try to memorize and meditate on the following Scripture to understand what Jesus can do for you and what you are supposed to be doing for the Lord:

"The Spirit of the Lord is on me, because he has anointed me to preach good news to the poor. He has sent me to proclaim freedom for the prisoners and recovery of sight for the blind, to release the oppressed, to proclaim the year of the Lord's favor." (Luke 4:18-19)

This Scripture is not just for Jesus but for all those who believe in Him. Jesus was anointed by the Holy Spirit to do the work of God. We are anointed by the Spirit to live a victorious life and serve the Lord. The Holy Spirit is a gift to those who have accepted Jesus as their personal Lord and Savior.

You receive this task when you become a Christian. This has to be your highest priority in life. We are made for the Lord. Our focus has to be to please Him.

(8) Practice silence and listen: If you have not experienced the Holy Spirit, try to listen to the Lord for one hour each day in silence. It's hard at first, but if you are persistent you will find this rewarding. It takes time to clear your mind and wait. You are telling God that what He has to say is important to you and that He is worthy of your time.

Prayer: "Lord Jesus, speak to me. I am listening." Then wait in silence, listen, and write a letter from Jesus. He will speak to you if you wait long enough. Solomon gave 1,000 offerings and God appeared in his dream. Be patient and wait. Eventually, you will hear from Him.

(9) Tell Jesus you love him: Make a habit of telling Jesus that you love him whenever you think about him. Love is a decision. You can show Jesus how important he is in your life by telling him that you care about him. You can think about him and tell him what's in your heart. He wants our deep, passionate love. He is not happy with us if we do our work without love for him. He sees your heart and knows if you are doing things out of love for him.

Prayer: "Lord Jesus, I love you more than anyone and anything. Let me love you and let love bring a smile to your face."

(10) Sing for Jesus: You can ask Jesus which song he wants you to sing for him. He may give you a song to sing. If you don't hear anything from him, sing a song that you think Jesus might like to hear from you. You can tell him, "Jesus, this song is for you," and sing silently or read it to Jesus if you are in a place where you can't sing.

"Let the word of Christ dwell in you richly as you teach and admonish one another with all wisdom, and as you sing psalms, hymns, and spiritual songs, do so with gratitude in your hearts for God. And whatever you do, whether in word or deed, do it all in the name of the Lord Jesus, giving thanks to God the Father through him." (Colossians 3:16-17)

(11) Write a love letter to Jesus: Thank Him for what He has done for you. Also, you can write a love letter from Jesus to help you understand how much God loves you.

(12) Learn to let go of distractions in your life: If anyone or anything is consuming your thoughts all the time, to the point that you can't focus on loving God, you need to give them to the Lord. Loving people and things more than God can become a distraction. Confess your sins and ask the Lord to help you.

Prayer: "Lord, help me not to love people or things more than I love you. I give all my loved ones and things to you for your care. Please take away all my sinful desires and obsessions. Help me plant the seed of love for you in my heart. I give all my loved ones to you for your work and for your glory. Help me to have the wisdom, knowledge, understanding, and revelation to solve my problems according to your will so that I can let go of my concerns and worries. Help me to love you and worship you."

(13) If you are hurting from grief and loss, you have to make a conscious decision to let go of your loved ones.

Prayer: "Holy Spirit, please heal my broken heart so that I can focus on loving God. Help me to see the big picture that you see. Help me to let go of my loved ones."

(14) Learn to listen to God's voice: There are four voices we hear in our minds: 1) Your voice; 2) other people's voices; 3) the devil's voice; 4) the Holy Spirit's voice. When the devil speaks to you, it's impure, sinful, and tempting. When you obey his voice you fall into sin and lose peace. You have to repent in order to find peace. The devil's voice is hurtful and negative. You will fall into sin if you accept that voice. Resist any negative voices. Use them as a trigger to pray for other people's salvation. The voice of the Holy Spirit is gentle and soft. His voice will comfort you and direct you to do good things. You will have peace and joy when you obey the Holy Spirit's voice.

Prayer: "Lord Jesus, help me to recognize your voice and obey you."

(15) Be obedient: There are four ways we do things: 1) my way; 2) other people's way; 3) the devil's way; 4) the Holy Spirit's way. The best course is to listen and follow the Holy Spirit in order to do things that please the Lord.

(16) Meditate on the Holy Communion to understand Jesus' love for you.

"While they were eating, Jesus took bread, gave thanks and broke it, and gave it to his disciples, saying, 'Take and eat; this is my body.' Then he took the cup, gave thanks and offered it to them, saying, 'Drink from it, all of you. This is my blood of the covenant, which is poured out for many for the forgiveness of sins.'" (Matthew 26:26-28)

Prayer: "Lord Jesus, help me to understand your love for me."

(17) Invite Jesus in: If you don't have a relationship with Jesus, invite Jesus into your life.

Prayer: "Lord Jesus, I give my life to you. Please come into my heart and my life. Forgive all my sins and cleanse my life so I can follow you. Bless me with the Holy Spirit. Jesus, guide and direct me to live a life that will please you. I pray this in Jesus' name. Amen."

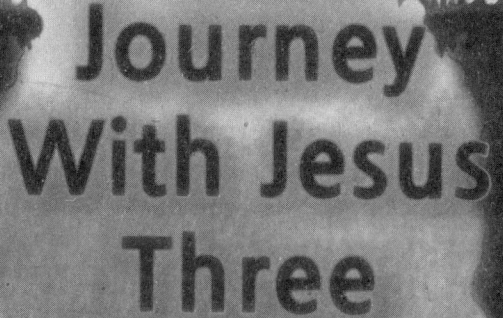

Journey
With Jesus
Three

How to Avoid the Pitfalls
of Spiritual Leadership

Yong Hui V. McDonald

INTRODUCTION

I started working as a chaplain at Adams County Detention Facility. Since then, the Lord has blessed me with a prison ministry beyond my wildest imagination. I am extremely grateful for these book projects, as well as having the privilege of meeting many spiritual leaders who serve Christ. I try to mentor the leaders, since the Lord has told me to train them from the beginning of my ministry. Many leaders in our facility are newly born Christians or recommitted people who want to make a difference in God's kingdom. They chair Bible studies and prayer meetings in their housing units and are effective in leading others to Christ.

It's a blessing to meet spiritual leaders who are eager to learn, but, as leaders, if they are not careful, they could fall into many dangerous holes and traps on their spiritual path. Not recognizing or being able to avoid these traps can lead us to fall into sin and away from the Lord. When this happens, the Lord is grieving. In addition, we lose our effectiveness in serving God when we fall into those holes. Even though I often shared my insights on what we need to watch out for as leaders, I never thought about writing this book until the Holy Spirit started directing me.

In 2012, Anthony, a bright young man who faithfully attended the chaplain's worship service, wanted to meet with me. He was eager to learn. This is what he wrote:

Hello Chaplain McDonald,

I feel so blessed by the church worship services and Bible studies. You asked what my calling was many times. I have been obedient to God's Word, law, and voice. I want to take the lead in my Christ-like walk and speak the good news.

I feel God has led me to come to you for help. Please strengthen me with your knowledge and wisdom as to the most important parts of being a strong influence in bringing others to Christ!!! A book, steps you write out, advice, and/or whatever the Lord has put on your heart to tell me will help me so much!!!

May God continue to bless you and your family. A true follower of Christ,

Anthony

I was glad that Anthony had the desire to know more about how to be an effective spiritual leader. I visited him and I wrote down the key points that I felt he should watch out for as a leader. After the meeting, as I got ready to leave, he said, "I would like to have it to look at, pray about, and to remind myself every day to stay on the right path."

"I will be glad to do that." I gave him a copy of what I wrote.

A week later, the Lord gave me the assignment to write a book to help leaders, people like Anthony, who are sincere in following Christ and wanting to serve but are in need of spiritual guidance. At first I resisted, as I was finishing another book and thinking about taking a break from writing for a while. Interestingly, this writing project request came the day I finished the book I was working on. I asked the Lord why I should write this book.

He spoke to me, "Do you remember what you have been telling others?"

What did I tell others? He reminded me that I used to tell others, "If you teach something and say it more than ten times, that means you have something to teach. You should make it into a book to help more people."

I learned that many people have lessons to teach others, but they do not believe that they can publish the lessons they have been teaching. The Lord taught me that my time is limited. I can teach individually and help some, but many more people would benefit if I wrote a book. Then, all I have to do is hand them a book and pray for them.

Another way the Lord encourages me to write occurs when I resist book assignments. He says, "If it will help only one person, you should do it."

As I thought about it, I realized I had told many others what I told Anthony. I should listen to myself and obey the Lord's leading in my book projects. My time is His time anyway, so I should follow the Holy Spirit's leading. Needless to say, I started this book.

I asked the Lord why I resist when He gives me a new assignment. He said, "You have not spent enough time with me, so you don't know what's in my heart. You come up with reasons why you shouldn't do them."

At that, I repented. "Please forgive me, Lord. I see that not spending enough time with you is another area Christians should pay attention to. Otherwise, we come up with excuses and reasons not to do things the way you want."

After that, I didn't have a grumbling heart. In fact, I started spending more time with the Lord as I began this book project. I felt overwhelmed with the task, so I started it many times but couldn't finish it. Interestingly, after the Lord called me to silent prayer and helped me to finish writing *Journey With Jesus Two in* February, 2014, He also guided me to write *Journey With Jesus Three* to help leaders recognize the dangerous holes they face. Praise God! I couldn't have written this if Jesus didn't help me. I give all the glory to him.

Journey With Jesus Three:
How to Avoid the Pitfalls of Spiritual Leadership

1. A Valley of Flowers

The girl was singing with the birds in the valley full of dandelions. There was tranquility in that place. Jesus looked at her with a smile as she blew on the dandelions and watched the seeds fly with the wind.

Jesus gently tapped her shoulder and said, "My loving daughter, I know you enjoy being here, but I need to show you some other places."

"Jesus, are you saying that you want to take me on another trip?"

"Yes, as I have told you, we pass through many places."

Jesus gave her a piece of cake and the girl ate it. It was very sweet and melted in her mouth. She smiled and said, "This is tasty!"

Jesus said, "My loving daughter, when you taste the love in my heart, it will be sweet like cake."

"My Lord, what are you trying to tell me?"

"I want you to write the next *Journey With Jesus.*"

The girl opened her eyes wide. "You want me to write another book? I thought I was finished with that story. Actually, I thought I was going to take a break for a while. You know I already have many other book projects."

"My loving child, you are able to do many good things, but you have to know my heart to be able to do what I want. That's important. Moses was taking care of sheep, but I had a task for him. I started sharing my heart with him and showed him my plans to save people from slavery. In *Journey With Jesus Two* you learned a lot about silent prayer, but this book will be about understanding my heart."

"My Lord, are you going to help me understand your heart?"

"Yes, but to understand my heart, you will first learn to understand your heart and the hearts of others."

"I am ready to follow you, Jesus."

"My loving child, your obedience makes me happy."

"Jesus, it's been more than two months since you asked me to silent prayer. Other than worship time, I cut off all music and I do not talk with other people except for my ministry. Do you still want me to continue with silent prayer?"

"I want you to keep up with silent prayer until you arrive at my Father's home. You cannot really understand my heart unless you take the time to listen."

"Lord, I like this silent prayer. Since I started it, I feel much better spiritually, emotionally, and physically."

"That's because you are being healed when you come into my presence. You will gain more strength as you continue to walk with me. To write this book, your silence is critical. Don't make a lot of plans, just try to listen to the Holy Spirit and obey."

"If writing this book is your will, then let your will be done in my life."

"Do you remember when I asked a while back for you to write a book to help the leaders?"

"Yes, Jesus. You asked me to write it a couple of years ago, but I didn't know where to start."

"My loving daughter, I will help you write it. This book will teach the spiritual leaders what they need to watch out for on their spiritual journeys. You will also learn from this."

"Thank you, Lord. I have had that book in the back of my mind."

"My loving daughter, even though you have been walking with me, you haven't really understood what is deep in my heart. That's why you didn't know how to start the book. I warn you that as you try to write this book, the spirit of pride will try to distract you, so be careful. Remember, you have to be humble in order to understand my heart."

"My Lord, help me to have a humble heart. I learned that it's easy to fall into the trap of pride when I work for you, especially on book projects. Too many people thank me and sometimes I feel special. I know it's wrong. If you didn't help me write, I wouldn't have anything to put on paper and I wouldn't have written any books. Please help me, Lord."

"I will help you, my child. Come and follow me. I have many places to show you."

The girl picked some flowers, got up, took Jesus' hand and followed him. Jesus looked pleased and the girl sang for him.

"Jesus, you are the most beautiful person I have ever met. Help me to know you better so I can experience your sweet loving heart."

2. A Hole of Pride

The girl and Jesus walked together quietly. After they passed the big valley of flowers, they approached a town that seemed familiar to her. It was her home town! Jesus took her to her house. The roof had been leaking the last time she was there, but she was happy to see that it was fixed.

When they walked into the house, it looked much better than before, but it was still not completely clean from the flood. One of the walk-in closets was filled with garbage instead of clothes.

The girl was dismayed. What she saw was that her spiritual house needed cleaning.

Jesus said, "My daughter, don't worry. The workers fixed the roof when you started silent prayer, but the inside still needs lots of work. As you keep praying and walking with me, the house will be repaired."

"Jesus, I didn't realize that I had so much junk in my closet. How did it get here?"

"You have been picking up lots of garbage throughout your ministry. Your focus should be on me, not yourself. It's easy to get caught up with caring about how other people see you. I want you to examine your heart when you hear from others. You have to realize how easy it is for my workers to fall into this trap. The spirit of pride is at work in many of my workers. They don't realize that what they need is my grace."

"Yes, it's your grace that saved me from many dangers and kept me alive to serve you. Now I realize that it's a privilege to serve you. Thank you, Lord, for your grace."

"My loving daughter, it's my grace that allows people to serve. Now, tell me, how has the spirit attacked you lately?"

"Actually, I thought I already had too many book projects, so I didn't start this one right away. Then, I heard the

devil whispering in my ear that I am special and that's why you gave me this book assignment. I knew immediately it was the spirit of pride trying to get me to fall into sin. This didn't happen to me with any other books. I went back to my notes and learned that you warned me about this. I realize now that an evil spirit tried to distract me from writing this book. However, you said you would help me write."

"My loving daughter, make sure that you give me the credit and glory for all your work. Then you won't fall into a trap. The devil knows that you will learn about my heart, so he is trying to distract you. To understand my heart, you have to clean your heart first. The devil doesn't want you to have a clean heart. He wants you to stay in your closet to get dirty and distracted. If that happens, you won't be able to do what I want you to do. If you don't recognize what the devil is doing, you will be deceived by it. You know that if you don't obey me, I can raise anyone to do what you do."

"Yes, Lord, it's your grace that asked me to write this book. Don't let the devil fool me into thinking that I can do it alone, since this isn't my idea. Whatever is making me fall down, please help me to repent."

"There are many dangers on the road for those who want to follow me. There are many holes as you walk, and this is one that people fall in. Many people get caught in this trap."

"Lord, how can we get out of the holes when we fall in?"

"Repenting is the only way. Proud people cannot see me or come to me for help. When my children start repenting, the Holy Spirit will start cleaning them and they will be able to climb out of the holes."

"Jesus, is there anything that I need to learn?"

"You have a lot to learn. I will show you the spiritual condition of your house."

3. A Hole of Not Praying

Jesus then led her to a closed door. Water was pouring out from under it. The girl was distraught.

"Lord, I thought the roof was fixed, but my house is still flooded!"

"My loving daughter, this water is coming out because there are many places that need to be fixed."

"Why is there so much damage to my house, Lord?"

"This is the spiritual condition of many of my children. They read the Bible but they don't apply it to their lives. They live in sin and they have no fear of God. When they are in that condition, the house's foundation is shaken and can be destroyed."

"My Lord, I am sorry. I read the Bible but didn't apply it to my life, especially the part to pray constantly. Sometimes I focused on my own comfort and forgot about others who need my care."

"What people don't realize is that I have given them gifts to be able to serve me, but they only serve themselves. Those who want to follow me have to deny their own desires. People need to seek God's kingdom and his righteousness first, but instead they seek their own gain and follow sinful desires."

"Jesus, please forgive me. I ignored your words for a long time. Please help me to obey you."

"I forgive you, daughter. You are starting to understand my heart. If you put me first and obey my word, you will not have a shaky foundation. This water is not from the roof but a cracked foundation."

"My Lord, please help me fix my house."

"As you decide to obey the word, your foundation will be fixed."

"Thank you, Lord. How can I help others who don't know that their spiritual houses have cracked foundations due to ignoring and disobeying the word of God?"

"My loving daughter, you need to pray for understanding of what I want you to do. You haven't been doing it. That's why I called you to silent prayer. Also, you need to pray that the Holy Spirit will give other leaders understanding, especially those working with you."

"Lord, please forgive me. I need to pray for others more than I have been. In fact, I focused only on my ministry and I

neglected prayers. Help me to pray more."

"How can I share my visions and dreams with you if you don't take the time to be with me? How can I help you do what I want you to do if you are not listening? How can I share my love with you if you don't come to me?"

"Lord, please forgive me for not spending enough time with you. Please help me to spend more time with you."

"Many of my workers are too busy with ministry work. They do not come to me or pray for people that they minister to. I want you to remember that without prayer, you can't help others effectively. Keep praying, my daughter. This is another hole many people fall into. People who rely on their own wisdom instead of praying fall into it."

"Thank you, Lord, for helping me to understand another hole that I have fallen into. Thank you for pulling me out of it by calling me to silent prayer."

"My daughter, there are many holes that my children need to understand, especially holes that spiritual leaders fall into. I will teach you what they are."

4. A Hole of Disobedience

The next room Jesus took her to had a door that didn't quite fit into the door frame; the door wouldn't close.

The girl asked, "Lord, why is this door twisted?"

Jesus said, "My daughter, many of my children's hearts resist me when I ask them to do something for my kingdom. They are the bosses of their ministries instead of me. They have disobedient hearts. They come up with excuses when I ask them to do something. They don't fully use their gifts. Even after they promise to serve me, their hearts are not with me. They try to do my work their own way. Why? Many of my workers don't understand my deep love and the plans I have for them. A person's heart is like this twisted door. People try to shape the door the way think it should be and it doesn't fit in the frame. After a while, the door cannot be used. It has become useless. That is the spiritual condition of some of my workers. I want you to empty your heart as much as possible in order to understand my heart of love. This is also an answer to your prayers, as you have been asking me to help you understand my heart."

"Jesus, I have been struggling with a disobedient heart for so long. I always have my own ideas and don't consider what you want me to do. Help me to obey you. Why is the lesson of obedience so hard?"

"My loving child, it's because you don't spend enough

time with me. Silent prayer will help you understand my heart. That will help you to be obedient. Do you see why you have a twisted door in your spiritual house?"

"I understand now, Lord. Please forgive me. I have been suffering from this disobedient heart for a long time. When you called me to ministry, I gave you many excuses. I didn't want to be a minister and I tried to run away from you, but you brought me back with your grace."

"I forgive you, daughter. When you understand my grace, you begin to have a humble heart. Now, I want you to make sure that you learn to be obedient. Many of my workers fall into the hole of disobedience."

"I was there for so long. The Holy Spirit called me to pray, but I fell into this hole and didn't do what I was supposed to. Lord, help me to not to get stuck in this hole anymore."

"My child, when people start using their gifts, the Holy Spirit will fill them with joy and fulfillment."

"I didn't know about my gifts. I didn't know what you had given me. How can I help others to know what they have received?"

"Keep encouraging them to use their gifts. Eventually, when people learn to understand my love and power, they can make the decision to obey me. You have many people working with you on book projects. Encourage them to use their gifts to build up my kingdom."

"Lord, I am amazed at how the Holy Spirit brings people to me to work on these projects to help prisoners and the poor. Help me to encourage them to use their gifts to their maximum abilities to save the lost, as well as for your glory."

"When people start using their gifts for me and my kingdom, they learn how to be obedient to my word. The twisted doors will be repaired. Keep praying to understand my deep love, then you will be able to obey the Holy Spirit's leading. Come, I have many things to show you."

5. A Hole of Worry and Fear

Before she left the house, the girl changed into a different pair of shoes, ones that looked more comfortable for the journey. At first they seemed fine, but as she followed Jesus, her feet started hurting. Every step became painful.

The girl stopped and said, "Lord Jesus, why are my shoes so tight? I thought they were fine when I started. Now they don't fit."

"My loving daughter, I have something to tell you. When you walk with me, you have to wear shoes that fit you so you will be comfortable."

"Lord, they didn't hurt before. I don't know what changed." The girl sat on the ground and took off her shoes. "I can't walk anymore."

"Child, you feel uncomfortable when I ask you to do something. Even though this project is going to help you, you have a feeling that it will overwhelm you. You need to let go of any worries regarding this project. You are not quite sure that you will be able to write this book because you have already forgotten that I am the one who will help you write. You won't have anything to write unless I guide your pen."

"Yes, Lord. You have seen my heart. I was wondering when you would stop piling on new projects. That's the reason I kept busy with other things."

"See, my child, the pain you are having with those shoes is your spiritual condition. Your heart is like those shoes. Your heart is not quite where I want it, and the shoes feel like they don't quite fit your feet. You struggle because you focus on other projects."

"I am sorry, Lord. Please forgive me. You are right. I have been reluctant to start this project. I felt I had too much to do already. I also need to work on my homework and other reports."

"My loving daughter, many of my workers fall into the

trap of worry and fear. They first say that they will do
something, then they feel overwhelmed by the task. Instead
of praying and doing the work, they do not move. They are
immobilized by the worry and fear that they are unable to do
what I want them to. You feel it's too much work, but I don't
ask you to do anything that you won't be able to complete.
Actually, I have already given you all the answers. When you
need to be reminded, come to me and I will help you."

"Lord, my heart is heavy with the task. What shall I do?"

"Child, I want you to give me your heart."

The girl thought that was a strange request. "My Lord,

I thought I gave you everything. Didn't I already give you my heart?"

"You said you were giving me your heart, but in reality you gave it to worry and fear. I want you to give me your heart so I can heal you."

The girl seemed to understand what he was saying. She said, "Is there anything that I am holding from you? Everything I have is yours, even my life. I give my heart to you so that you can help me."

"My loving daughter, I will help you."

"Let me have your heart and your peace."

"My child, to understand the depth of my heart, you must learn not only it's joy, but it's sorrow as well. Sometimes you will understand my pain through other people's pain. That's what my heart is."

"Jesus, if that is the only way to understand your heart, help me to comprehend your sweet loving heart and to bear that pain with your strength. Is there anything else that I need to learn?"

"I am pleased with your willingness to learn from me."

"Lord, help me to learn to love you with all my heart, mind, soul, and strength. Help me to do what you want me to do."

Jesus' face was bright with a loving smile. "To love me with all your heart, you have to understand my heart. Now, I want you to get up and walk. See if your shoes fit you or not."

The girl got up and realized that now the shoes fit her perfectly. She danced and said, "Lord Jesus, thank you so much for helping me to have comfortable shoes. You work wonders in my life."

Jesus said, "If your heart is ready to do what I want you to do, it will be easy to follow without a struggle. You will be able to focus on what I want you to do when you let go of your own plans and ideas. When you give me your heart,

I can heal your disobedience. This is another hole many of my children fall into. They give their hearts to worry and fear instead of me."

The girl sang and followed Jesus, "My dear Jesus, thank you for helping me to realize that I was dwelling on worry and fear. I give you my heart so I can experience healing from you. Help me to do the things you ask me to do with joy. Don't let me fall into the hole of worry and fear again. I give you my heart so I can love you."

"My daughter, recognizing why you struggle begins the heart's healing process. I will help you to have a willing heart. Follow me."

The girl followed Jesus and started dancing for him. She knew Jesus was happy when she danced for him.

6. A Hole of Following Blind Leaders

Jesus took her to the busy streets of a city where many people were walking. Among them, two men walked close together. The one leading the way was blind.

Jesus said, "My loving child, I want you to know that there are many spiritually blind leaders who think that they know everything. They don't know my heart. They may have wisdom, but that wisdom is not from me. In fact, these blind leaders persecute my workers who can actually see. I want you to be aware of this so you are not discouraged when others misunderstand you."

"Lord Jesus, why is the blind man up front and the other man following? Can he not see that the leader is blind?"

"Many of my children are like babies who do not know what spiritual discernment is. They need to listen to me but they don't. Instead, they follow people instead of me. What happens when someone follows a blind leader? They are unable to find the right path. This has happened to you before, don't you remember?"

"Oh, Lord, now I remember what happened. I was with many respectable people who didn't believe that there was a hell. I started doubting your words and I started backsliding after spending time with them. They were very kind and nice people. They had high moral standards and they loved people. I didn't see anything wrong with them, but they didn't believe the word of God completely. Their interpretation of the Scripture was different from what I have learned is true."

"Now you see it. People who do not believe my words are spiritually blind. They don't understand my heart or the reality of hell. Why would I die on the cross for the world if

196

there was no hell and punishment for those who don't believe in me?"

"Lord, I am sorry I listened to those misguided people. Please help me not to become a blind leader or follow one."

"The reason I want to share my heart with you is so you can help many of my children who follow worldly spiritual leaders. They put their trust in the wisdom of the world instead of me."

"Please help me to have spiritual discernment as to whom I should follow."

"My loving daughter, you need to follow me and learn from me. Then you will have the wisdom to teach others. Just be aware that many leaders don't trust my words. Even though they say that they work for me, they preach their own wisdom, which doesn't have life."

"What shall I do? How can I help others?"

"Preach the gospel. Teach them what I have said. Teach them to prepare for the future. Everyone will be judged according to what they believe and what they have done. You need to keep teaching them to obey my words. Many of my workers fall into the trap of relying on their own wisdom. That's why I called you to listen, so you can teach my words to the hungry people."

"Thank you, Lord Jesus. Are there any other lessons I need to learn from this?"

Jesus smiled. "My loving daughter, I am glad that you asked that. There is another lesson in this. I don't want you to be discouraged when others misunderstand your walk with me."

"Lord, I am learning that there are some who misunderstand me, even in my silent prayer. I tried to explain, but they still didn't understand me."

"That's why I am telling you that you should not mentor anyone unless the Holy Spirit asks you to. Your time with me becomes distracted when you try to help too many people. If you obey me, I will take care of everything. If you try to please other people, you will end up in a hole of following blind leaders."

"Am I in that hole?"

"No, not any more, but you were a while back. Can you remember?"

"Jesus, I can't think of anything now. Can you help me?"

"The time you tried to help others but they ended up turning against you."

"Oh, that time. I understand what you are saying. I thought I was helping others but they took advantage of my kindness. At the time, I trusted people more than I should have and became upset and angry. You helped me to forgive them. Thank you."

"Whatever you do, even when it's good, ask the Holy Spirit before beginning from now on. Also, when you help someone, don't expect anything from them. Just share what I have given you. In that way, you won't get hurt."

"Lord, help me to have the wisdom to handle things in your way instead of mine."

"My loving daughter, you are learning! You must follow the Holy Spirit, not your own wisdom."

"Thank you, Lord Jesus, for this lesson. I was following blind leaders at times and I didn't even realize it. That's how I got hurt."

"My child, some of my workers do not have a clear conscience. They do not have a fear of the Lord. Stay away from these people. They create distractions and turmoil in your journey."

"Lord, help me to have a clear conscience. Open my eyes so I don't fall into these holes."

"Keep your eyes on me, listen, and follow. Otherwise, you can be blinded by worldly standards and your own wisdom. Avoid spiritually blind people who try to influence you. I want you to boldly tell others about my love so that they can find me and follow me."

"Lord, how can I do it? I want to do what you have planned for me."

"Remember the Scripture of Jeremiah 1:17-19, where it says, 'Get yourself ready! Stand up and say to them whatever I command you. Do not be terrified by them, or I will terrify you before them. Today I have made you a fortified city, an iron pillar and a bronze wall to stand against the whole land —against the kings of Judah, its officials, its priests and the people of the land. They will fight against you but will not overcome you, for I am with you and will rescue you,' declares the LORD."

"Lord, it seems the task is too great. This Scripture sounds like having a battle with many people. You know I don't want to have conflict with anyone."

"My loving daughter, I want you to get ready. The devil knows how to disrupt my children when I give them an assignment. As long as you ask for my wisdom, you will not be hurt by others. Prayer engages you in a spiritual battle. The more you pray, the more able you will be to fight with my wisdom and strength. If you keep praying, the spirit of pride will not attack you. I will be with you and help you share with others."

"Lord, your will be done in my life. I already gave you my life, so use me to the maximum for your glory."

"You are beginning to understand what I am trying to say. I have to share my heart for you to understand it. Nothing comes from you when I share my heart."

"Thank you, Jesus, for warning me to be humble. I give you all the glory for everything. I give you the glory for what you share with me now and in the future."

7. A Hole of Prejudice

"My loving child, I will bless you through this project.

That's my grace. What you experience will be from me."

"Thank you. What do you want me to do?"

"Extend your silent prayer, no matter what others say. I will protect you from those who don't understand. It's time to do some cleansing of the heart. I want you to work on purification."

"How do I do that?"

"Do you remember when I told you to think that all the young people are like your beloved son?"

"Yes, Lord, but what are you trying to say?"

"I want you to think that all the people in the world are people that I love. I love people so much that I gave them my life. I want you to have that understanding and I want you to have that love."

"Lord, I really need your help in that area. Please help me to love everyone as you love them."

"My loving daughter, you asked me how you can be cleansed. That's one area that needs cleansing. Your ministry is not just for the people you want to minister to, but all people. Do you remember when you only thought about prisoners at your facility and I told you that your vision was too small? That vision has to be enlarged in order for you to have a clean heart."

"Lord, I still don't understand what a clean heart has to do with this bigger vision of loving everyone."

"That's because you don't understand my big heart. This is just the beginning of your learning about my heart. I love everyone, not just certain people. This is a lesson you need to learn from me."

"Oh, I get it Lord. Your heart is big and you love everyone. That's the concept that I need to work on. I need to have an open mind."

"You said you want to understand my heart. Understanding isn't good enough. I want you to have my heart so you can love everyone, not just those you choose."

"Thank you, Lord Jesus, for helping me to recognize my limited understanding of who I need to focus on ministering to. You are telling me that my ministry focus needs to expand."

"That's it. When you have my heart, people can be freed from prejudice and change their understanding of their mission. Many church leaders have a very narrow perception of ministry. That's because they don't understand my big heart, which embraces everyone."

"Now I get it! When you called me to the ministry, I thought I would only be working with Americans, but you told

me that you wanted me to work with Koreans too. I didn't want to work with Koreans because I had been away from that society for a long time. Recently, though, I have been working with Koreans, and it has been a blessing. Lord, how can I have your love and a vision like yours?"

"Keep practicing silent prayer. Listen to my heart, then you will be able to embrace everyone with my love. As you pray more, my vision becomes your vision. Many of my leaders have not learned to embrace everyone with their mission projects. That's because they don't understand my heart. Their visions are too small, just like when you only thought about people where you work. I told my disciples to go and make believers of all nations, but many are satisfied with missions in their own home churches. People don't realize this, but they seek their own comfort and only want to help people they care for. You need to purify your heart by recognizing that my vision is bigger. I want you to help people enlarge their visions by breaking down prejudice. First, you need to master this to be able to teach others. Come and follow me, I have many things to show you."

"Lord, I am beginning to see how difficult it is to understand your heart. I used to think only about my own comfort and family. That's why I didn't want to sacrifice myself for ministry."

"The hole that's apparent in many of my workers is that they are satisfied with only taking care of churchgoers. This is a trap of comfort that many fall into. They ignore the Holy Spirit. When that happens, people do not reach out to others. Instead, they burrow into their own holes of comfort."

"Lord, help me to have your heart and have the courage to do what you want me to do. Help me not to stumble into a hole of comfort and become trapped into thinking that I am doing fine, when in reality I am not."

"My loving daughter, learn from me. Keep listening."

8. A Hole of Loving Money

Jesus and the girl were passing a town when she heard that one of her old friends had robbed a bank. She hadn't seen him for a while but she was concerned about him.

To her surprise, the man who robbed the bank came to see her. He took a fistful of money out of his backpack and said, "Take this money and use it."

In disbelief she pleaded, "Turn yourself in. You will get caught eventually. It's better if you do it now."

The man didn't seem to understand her and he left. The girl was grief-stricken and wept. She turned to Jesus.

"My Lord, what's happening here? I thought he would listen to me. I feel sorry for him. I don't know what to do."

"My daughter, many of my workers have problems with money. They love money more than they love me. Some left the ministry because they fell into the hole of loving money more than anything. When that happens, they don't just rob other people, they steal from me."

"How can people steal from you?"

"There are many things that I give to people to share with others. Money is one of them, along with talents and time. The most critical thing is their time. You are shocked when you see people rob others, but I see people steal from me everyday. Unfortunately, they don't seem to realize it. They don't ever pay back what they owe."

"Lord, I am sorry. Please explain some more."

"I created the world and its people. They are mine, but many don't realize that what I have given them is mine, not theirs. I gave them life and all they have. I created them for my glory, to praise me and love me. I love them. I showed them the extent of my love by dying on the cross for their sins. Many do not have the heart to give back what they owe—their lives, which is their time. What I really want from them are their hearts. I want them to comprehend my love, but they don't come to me to understand it. There are some who recognize it and spend time with me, but most of them, even many of my workers, use my time for their own selfish reasons. Also, I gave people gifts to build up my kingdom, but they are not interested in the things that I want them to do. They use what they have for their own gain."

The girl cried, "Lord, I am sorry. I have done wrong many times. I neglected my devotional time with you even after I started ministry. I thought leading worship services was good enough for you."

"My loving child, leading and worshipping is important, but what's most important for you is spending time alone with me. You have to make the time to be alone with me to understand my heart and my love. When you lead worship, you need to follow the Holy Spirit, but you still think about the people you minister to, so you cannot focus on me completely."

"Lord, why didn't I understand earlier that you want me to lead worship services for others, but also to worship on my own? The Holy Spirit asked me for years to spend more time in prayer, but I ignored it. I thought leading worship services was good enough for my walk with you. You know how many worship services I lead every week."

"You are doing what I called you to do when you lead worship, but I also want your undivided attention during personal devotional time so that I can converse with you."

"Jesus, I am sorry. I know I need to love you with all my heart, soul, mind, and strength. I didn't realize that my personal devotion is what you really want."

"My loving child, I want you to come to my presence not just when you worship with others, but by yourself everyday as well. Then you will eventually learn how to love me with all your heart, mind, soul, and strength."

"Thank you, Lord Jesus, for teaching me how to love you. I want to love you now more than ever."

"Now you know why the Holy Spirit was asking you to spend five hours with me everyday. Previously, you answered by saying that you spent so much time leading worship that you thought that replaced your intimate time with me."

"Lord, I'm sorry. I am getting it now. You want my total, undivided attention focused on loving you. Spending time in personal devotion is what you want."

Jesus said, "Many people are stealing my time and using it for their own gain. I don't want you to be like that. The more you spend time with me, the more you will understand what I am trying to tell you. As you get to know my heart, you will learn about my sweet presence. I love you, so I want to spend time with you alone. This is not just for you, but everyone who wants to understand my love and wants to love me. They need to know that everything they have is mine and it's a gift to them. Life is a testing ground to see how much people learn to recognize that what they have is mine. They need to use it for my glory, not their own."

"Lord, thank you so much for teaching me this lesson. I ask your forgiveness for neglecting to spend time with you. Help me to spend more time with you so I can get to know your heart."

"Now you can see why I want you to make sure that you don't have anyone that you talk to more than me or anyone who is closer to you than me. If you do, you forget about me. Your ministry became like that in the past, so you need to watch out."

"Jesus, what else do you want me to know?"

"Everything you have is mine, so follow the Holy Spirit's leading. Use it for my glory. I also want you to teach others to use their gifts to serve me and help others."

"Thank you, Lord, for your teaching on this subject. Help me not to steal your time and gifts for my own selfish gain, but to use them for your glory."

"My loving daughter, it makes me happy to see that you are learning my heart."

9. A Hole of Noises

Jesus said, "My loving daughter, I'm looking for people who can understand my heart of love and compassion so they can comprehend my pain for others. That way they can deliver my people from misery."

"My Lord, what shall I do?"

"Keep preaching the gospel to those who have not heard it or have a difficult time hearing it because of their harsh living conditions. That's why your books need to go to places where poor and hungry people are. You cannot help others unless you understand their pain. To do that, you need to spend more time in silence listening to my heart. Many of my workers are listening to lots of noises in the world and they do not hear what I'm trying to tell them. That is another hole many people fall into. When they do, they cannot hear me. Come and follow me."

Jesus took her to a hole filled with loud music where many people were dancing. Some people passed out and some attacked others, but no one could hear the cries of others.

The girl shook her head and said, "Lord, what you show me is happening in many places. People are busy watching TV and listening to music. Many are not able to listen to you. You know that I cannot ask them to shut off their distractions. You asked me to shut off all of my music except for during worship services, but I feel this task is too big for me. How can I tell others of the dangers of worldly noises? People don't see it as a big problem in their spiritual journey. Why do you choose a person like me to write a book about these holes?"

"When you asked, you said you wanted to have more love for me. That's where this book originated. In order for you to have more love for me, you have to understand my deep love for you and others. In order to love me, people need to hear about the distractions."

"Thank you, Lord. Now I understand why you don't want me to hear too many noises, even when they are good. Understanding your heart is hard when I listen to too many noises. A while back, you asked me to give you my heart. I wondered why, because I thought I already gave you everything."

"My loving daughter, you have given your heart to me, but not completely. Most of the time you try to focus on what you want to do. When I tried to help you write this book, you resisted because of your own desires. You have your own plans. That's why I asked you to give me your heart. You try to do good things, but many times even the good things become distractions when I am leading you to do something. Unless you recognize that, you cannot truly follow me. Many of my children are distracted by everyday life. They believe they make the best decisions for me, but, in reality, they ignore my plans for them. That's why I asked you to give me your heart, so you will comprehend that writing this book is my plan for you."

"Lord, you are great! I realize that what you are telling me is true. At the beginning of my ministry, you told me that I always resisted your plans. That's still happening. I am sorry. Please forgive my reluctant attitude. Please change my heart so I can do your will. Help me to follow your plans for me, and to make them my highest priorities."

"My child, I want you to recognize that distraction in your life is not just found in your resisting spirit, but anything that diminishes your devotional time in prayer. Your ministry became a distraction for a while until I pointed it out to you. You were too busy. Even though your were working for me, you neglected spending time with me. Don't let any distractions come between us. Distractions can be people or things. You have to listen to me to learn what distracts you. There is nothing more important than understanding my love. That will help you to have more love for me, if that's what you truly want."

"Lord, help me not to get distracted by anyone or anything, even noises. I want to focus on spending time with you and loving you. Let me understand your deep love."

"If you watch out for those distractions, you will be able to learn what's in my heart."

"How can I hear from you more?"

"The more you spend time in silence, the more you will be able to understand my heart. Many people suffer from the distraction of too much noise. They cannot hear me because of other sounds."

"Thank you, Lord. Help me to practice silent prayer more."

10. A Hole of Loving Others More Than Jesus

They were walking past a mountain when a woman's weeping sound echoed from the cliffs. The girl tried to figure out where the cry was coming from. It was coming from the ground! When she got close, she realized that there was a deep hole a woman had fallen into.

The woman said, "Lord, please forgive me for failing you. I wanted to serve you, but too many things were happening. My mother died and I didn't think I could go on. Then I had financial problems and my children needed me."

The girl turned to Jesus, "Lord, what's happening here? I hear many voices echoing, but there is only one woman here. It feels like there are many people in this mountain."

"My daughter, this is a mountain of distraction. Many people who are called to serve me go past this mountain. There are many holes that people can fall into and get trapped. They can't get out, so they cannot walk with me or serve me."

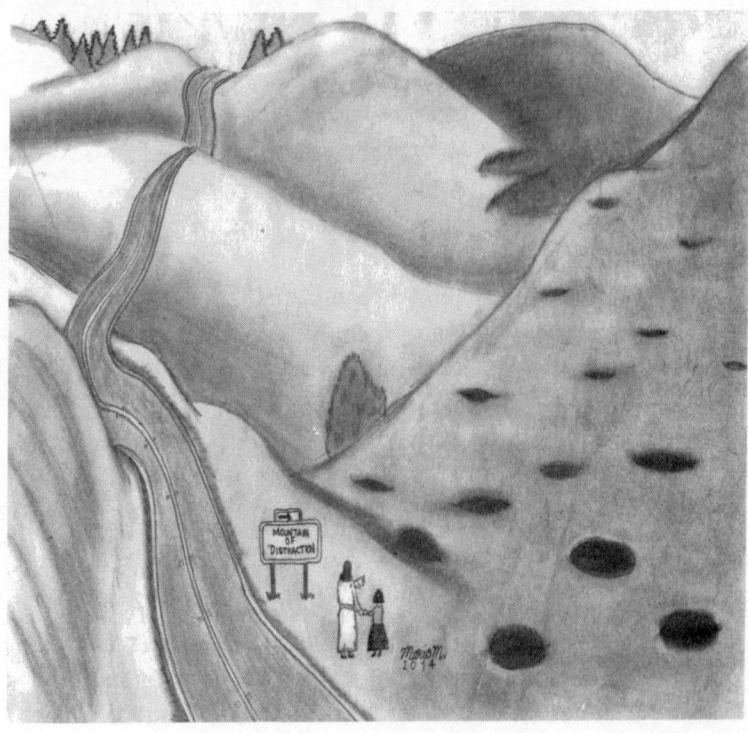

"Why can't you save them, Lord? Can't you pull them out?"

"The Holy Spirit can pull them out when they repent and make the decision to follow me. Many feel bad that they don't follow me, but they go back to their lives and forget about my calling. This woman was called to serve in Africa as a missionary but when hardships came, she gave up on following me. She loved her family more than me. She still lives in misery because she never got out of this hole to face life's problems. She laments everyday, but does not repent or make an effort to follow me."

"Lord, it seems easy to fall into this kind of trap."

"You fell into one of these holes before. I will show you the hole where you were trapped."

As they walked along, there was a hole with a little girl playing with dolls in it. The girl realized that she was seeing herself. "There! I see it, Lord. Why did I stay in that hole so long? It's just toys that I was playing with."

"My daughter, your distraction was yourself. You loved yourself more than me. You also thought that working for me was worthless. People who don't value me don't value ministry. You thought that playing with dolls, which was following your own plans, was better than following me."

212

"Lord, please forgive me. I now understand why I struggled so much when you called me to ministry."

"People who love anyone or anything more than me cannot follow me. Instead, they fall into these holes."

"Lord, please help me to understand these holes so I can watch out for them. I don't want to fall into sin any longer."

"My loving daughter, there are many holes in this mountain. Many fall into these holes because they are not prepared for the journey. They recognize where they are, but they don't know how to get out. I want you warn people about these dangers so they can avoid them. When you fall into a hole, it takes a while to get out. It's easy to fall into the holes when you don't know the dangers you face on the journey."

11. A Hole of Disappointments

As they walked along, the girl heard a man's voice saying, "I give up." This voice echoed off the mountain.

Jesus looked sad. "This is a hole of temptation to quit serving me. When people face difficulties, they decide to follow the world instead of me. It grieves me to see that my people are in misery here. This man is a minister, but felt rejected by some of his congregation. He lost hope in ministry because he dwelled on the situation and people more than on me."

"How can he get out of this hole of disappointment?"

"All he has to do is repent for relying on his own strength instead of the Holy Spirit. He needs to find hope and strength through the Holy Spirit. If he turns to me, I will give him the strength to get out, but he is not willing to do that."

"Lord, this mountain of distraction seems to be hard for people to pass by without falling into holes."

"Actually, people who follow me closely and listen to the Holy Spirit's guidance will be warned of the holes. They can be avoided, but many do not pay attention to the Holy Spirit. Instead, they follow their own plans. That's another lesson you need to learn."

"Lord, help me to hear and obey the voice of the Holy Spirit so I can avoid these holes."

"If you pay attention to the Holy Spirit, he will help you get out, even if you fall into a hole."

"Lord, now I know why I felt despair. I didn't see the power of God for a long time. I didn't know that the Holy Spirit has the power to transform lives. While writing the first *Journey With Jesus,* I saw the mighty transforming power of the Holy Spirit. How can I continue to follow the Holy Spirit's leading?"

"My loving child, keep praying. You will be able to hear the voice of the Holy Spirit clearly."

12. A Hole of Excuses

As they walked along, the girl heard a voice saying, "I cannot do this, Lord."

Jesus and the girl stopped in front of a hole where a woman sat praying. "Lord, I cannot do it. Why do you call me? I don't think I can do it." The woman was sobbing. She kept saying the same thing over and over again.

Jesus explained, "Many of my children say that they love me and want to serve me. Then when I call them, they come up with many reasons not to follow."

"Lord, I was in that hole for a long time myself. I remember giving you many excuses. I thought it would be better for you to pick others more capable of doing the work for you. One of the reasons was that English is my second language. You changed my heart to follow you by helping me to understand the power of the Holy Spirit."

Jesus smiled, "I know how you felt. I don't call people because they are equipped to do my work. I call them because they know that they don't have the power to do my work. They have to rely on the Holy Spirit's power. This woman is only looking at herself from the human perspective. She doesn't believe in my power to transform people."

"My Lord, how can people avoid falling into this hole?"

"They have to have more confidence in me and the power of the Holy Spirit. Many forget that I gave them the Holy Spirit to help them serve me. Remind them that they are not doing it with their own wisdom or power, but mine."

"Lord, help me to have confidence in your power so I can do what you want me to do. Help me to have confidence in you so that I can confess like Paul, 'I can do all things through Jesus Christ who strengthens me.'"

"Keep reminding others that all they need to do is obey their call."

13. A Hole of Self-Reliance

The girl was walking through some bushes when she heard the echoes of a big sigh. Then, a voice came from a hole, "I feel trapped. I worked for 15 years in ministry and I don't know how I can handle 15 more."

The words "I feel trapped" kept echoing through the air. The girl looked down into a deep hole where a man was fishing on dry ground. He kept casting the fishing line, but there wasn't water or fish anywhere in sight.

He said, "I can't believe I can't catch any fish."

The girl thought it was strange that he didn't realize that he was on dry ground.

Jesus said, "This man has no idea why he is not able to catch fish."

"Why, Lord?"

"Because he is spiritually blind. He cannot see that he is on dry ground. He thinks he should be catching fish, since he believes he is in a lake. He is not able to see that he needs to find the right place. First, his eyes have to be opened to see what reality is."

"Lord, how can he open his eyes? Can you help him see that he is in the wrong place to fish?"

"His blindness came on when he thought only of his own comfort. He was not willing to go out and explore different places to catch fish. Instead, he kept staying home. He enjoyed his own games and ungodly things, which made him blind to my power. He doesn't repent, but watches and reads worldly things which are made by ungodly people."

"Why, Lord, do people fall into this hole? Doesn't he know that he is trapped?"

"My daughter, many of my workers are in this condition. They enjoy worldly, sinful things and enjoy what they see, but they don't hear the cry of the needy. He doesn't want to hear the cry of others."

"Lord, this is very hard for me. At one point, I didn't think about others who suffer either. However, I wondered why people were not being saved. I didn't make any effort to help others find God or to help the needy. Please help me to avoid this trap."

"It's easy to fall into the trap of seeking your own comfort. When you feel like you have done enough for others, that's when you start making plans for yourself to be comfortable."

"Why, Lord, is it wrong to make plans like that?"

"People make plans for their own selfish reasons. They are not a part of my plan. People who make plans for themselves fall into to this trap."

"Lord, teach me so that I don't fall into the trap of comfort or think that I have done enough."

"My loving daughter, you are on the way to learning how to avoid these holes. When you spend time with me, the Holy Spirit will warn you of them. I called you to silent prayer so you could understand what I am trying to tell you. You were comfortable with yourself and made plans without thinking about my plans for you. You need to watch out when you make plans by yourself. This man made plans by himself and though he served me for 15 years, his ministry wasn't fruitful because he didn't listen to me."

"How can this man live the next 15 years not feeling trapped?"

"When he finally recognizes that his plans don't work, humbles himself, and starts praying that he will understand my plans for him. Then the Holy Spirit will lead him to a place where he can be fruitful."

"Thank you, Lord Jesus. Help me to humble myself and follow the Holy Spirit's leading so I can have a fruitful ministry."

14. A Hole of Loving the World

The girl continued to follow Jesus. This time, she heard someone saying, "Wow, this tastes great!"

The voice was coming from a hole where a man was drinking. Next to him was a bottle that had baby worms in it. The man had a cup that was covered with little black bugs, but he kept drinking. He seemed to be unaware of what he was consuming.

The girl couldn't believe what she saw and turned to Jesus, "My Lord, what's happening to this man? Can't he see that he is drinking bugs?"

Jesus replied, "My loving daughter, he is spiritually blind and thinks that it's alright to live in sin."

"Lord, why does he think that way?"

"People who immerse themselves with impure thoughts can be spiritually blind. They cannot see or feel. What they drink will eventually hurt them. Anyone who lives in sin with lustful thoughts falls into this hole. They don't even know that what they are doing will bring disaster."

"What is the problem?"

"My child, this happens to many people who live an impure lifestyle. They believe that it's alright to live in sin, and they hurt themselves and others. They love pleasure more than me. Remember the Scriptures. 'But mark this: There will be terrible times in the last days. People will be lovers of themselves, lovers of money, boastful, proud, abusive, disobedient to their parents, ungrateful, unholy, without love, unforgiving, slanderous, without self-control, brutal, not lovers of the good, treacherous, rash, conceited, lovers of pleasure rather than lovers of God—having a form of godliness but denying its power. Have nothing to do with them.'" (2 Timothy 3:2-5)

"Jesus, how can they get out of this hole?"

"Only repenting and changing their lifestyles can restore them to be able to see the truth."

"Lord, please help them to understand what sin is and learn to love you more than pleasure."

"My loving daughter, the truth will set them free from sinful desires. First, they have to want to live a pure life and turn their hearts to me. Unless they start repenting, they will not see the truth."

"Lord, how can I make sure that I live a pure life that is pleasing to you?"

"My child, look up to me when you are tempted. Ask me for direction when you face temptation. Come to me and be in my presence to be purified. Then, you will be cleansed and have a pure heart. Many enjoy living sinful lives because sin seems to be sweet at first, then it turns bitter, poisons their conscience, and makes their hearts sick. If they turn to me and repent, they will be forgiven and healed."

"Jesus, help me to have a pure heart so I don't get sick."

"Keep following me, then your heart will be purified. Come, I will show you what you need to see."

15. A Hole of Anger

The trip was long. There were different echoes as they passed through different places. This time, the girl heard people screaming at each other from a hole. When she got close to the hole, she saw two men in it throwing rocks and cussing at each other.

Jesus turned to the girl. "My loving daughter, many people never learn how to create peace and they throw rocks at each other. These two men are leaders, but they don't have any love or respect for each other. They have been fighting in the church. One is a minister and the other one is also a leader, but they both have a spirit of anger and fight over insignificant things. They both think they are right. In the process, they forget to save others who are lost and dying. They focus instead on whether or not they are right and the other one is wrong. Many of my children fall into a trap of self-righteousness and waste time and energy. People have a spirit of aggression and they don't know how to solve problems peacefully. These men ended up in a hole. That's what the devil wants. Those who keep fighting forget about me and the task of saving people who are lost."

"My Lord, how do I develop a peaceful spirit?"

"I want you to spend less time with people who have a spirit of aggression so you can avoid falling into sin and the hole of anger."

"My Lord, how can I avoid people like that?"

"My child, people with aggression are quick to throw their anger at others. They are the ones you need to avoid."

"Wouldn't it be great if I could help them let go of their

anger instead of avoiding them?"

"You can help them, but they need to realize that there is a problem first. Sometimes these people are already in this hole and they pull you down into it with them."

"Jesus, I need you to help me have the discernment to avoid aggressive people that will pull me into the hole of misery."

"It's very important to listen to the Holy Spirit when you have problems with aggressive people."

"Jesus, let me have the wisdom to rely on the Holy Spirit to resolve problems. How can these people get out of the hole?"

"All they need is to be cleansed from their sins through repentance. Then I will give them insight on how to change their hearts. The Holy Spirit will heal their wounds and help them to be loving and gentle. When that happens, violence can be changed to gentleness. Everything is possible with my power."

"So why do I need to avoid this kind of people?"

"You can be gentle with them, but they will wear you down to the point that you will waste a lot of time with them instead of spending time with me. Then you can't do what I want you to do. People who do not learn to have love and respect for others will pull you down into the hole of anger."

"Jesus, what if the person who has an angry spirit is someone I am ministering to? What shall I do? How can I avoid them?"

"You need to spend more time praying to see the whole picture in order to understand why that person is aggressive. You shouldn't be close to anyone who is filled with an angry spirit or you will become like them."

"Jesus, are you saying that if I try to change a person, I may end up falling into a hole?"

"Yes, their purpose is to pull you down into the hole they are in. They don't even know that they are in the hole. They think that what they are doing is right."

"Lord, thank you so much. Now, I remember a time that I met a person who didn't have any respect for others. He treated me badly and I acted just like him. I got mad and angry and called him names."

"That's what I am talking about, daughter. People with a violent temper will pull you down into the hole they are in."

"Yes, Lord. You're right. I didn't realize that the man had pulled me into the hole of anger. I couldn't get out of the hole for a long time because I found it hard to forgive him. Eventually, you asked me to forgive him and I climbed out of the hole with your help."

"My loving child, this is a hole many people continuously fall in whether they are in church or at home. People have no love or respect for each other, so they keep criticizing each other and fighting. Many of my workers are hurting because they are in the hole of anger and aggression. People who have disrespectful, judgmental attitudes fall into this hole. Pray that people will be united through love and forgiveness. Stay away from people who are angry, judgmental, and critical of others. They will become distractions on your journey with me."

"Lord, please help me not to be quick to anger, judgmental, or critical of others. Help me to have love and respect for everyone. Help me to have the wisdom to stay away from people who could disturb my walk with you."

"People who do not have love and respect for others do not create peace. Rather, they cause turmoil in other people's lives. Those are the people you need to avoid."

"I want peace more than anything, Lord."

"My loving daughter, I give you peace. My peace is what you need. Avoid people who disturb your peace."

"Thank you, Lord, for giving me peace. Let your peace be mine always."

"You know where to find peace."

"Jesus, spending time with you and listening to your loving voice is the way to keep peace in my heart."

"My loving daughter, that's why I asked you not to have anyone whom you spend more time with than me. I told you not to allow anyone closer than me. Then you will have my peace. Even if others are kind and gentle, they cannot give you what I can give you. Others will take away your peace if you spend too much time with them. I can give you peace, perfect peace. You can keep this peace if you spend time with me. I called you to silent prayer so you could be filled with my love and peace."

"Lord, I want your peace all the time."

"My loving child, you are learning what's important on your journey. People need me to have my peace. My loving words will restore their wounds and bring them peace. From now on, I want you to spend more time with me so you can do what I want you to do. Don't waste your time. Time is short. There are many who need my peace, but don't know what peace is about. When they find me, they will find peace. Preach the gospel. When you plant the seed of the gospel with your books, many people will be able to find me. Then my peace will be theirs."

"Lord Jesus, please help me to walk with you so I can keep this peace."

"My child, as long as you are walking with me, you will have it. Don't just keep my peace, but spread it to others by spreading the gospel. Wherever the gospel seed is planted, the spirit of peace will sprout."

The girl exclaimed. "Lord Jesus, you are the Prince of Peace. I love you and praise you."

The girl started dancing for Jesus and he was pleased.

16. A Hole of Demons

As they walked along, the girl wondered how many holes

were in the mountain. For a while, everything was quiet, so she thought maybe she had seen all of the holes. Suddenly, though, she heard someone crying out in pain.

This hole had a man in it who covered his face while a demon whipped him. The man being beaten didn't fight back or try to stop the demon from whipping him.

Jesus looked very sad and said, "My loving daughter, many of my workers don't know how to fight the spiritual battle."

The girl was in shock and said, "Why doesn't this man fight back?"

"That's because his spiritual eyes are blind and he cannot see what's happening. He thinks he knows the Bible but he doesn't believe that there are spiritual beings or spiritual attacks."

The girl couldn't understand. "Why can't he see the demon?"

"Many of my children don't see them, but they are there. They can feel the attacks, but since they don't believe that there are tormenting demons, they think they are just in pain."

"Lord, that was my condition before I learned about spiritual warfare. I didn't know why I was hurting. I was tormented by the devil, but the Bible taught me how to fight the devil in your name. You released me from all the pain caused by the tormenting demon's attacks. How can I help others who are suffering from demonic attacks?"

"First, pray for people who are suffering from spiritual attacks, then try to teach others about spiritual warfare. The sooner people are aware of this spiritual war and begin to fight the devil, the quicker they will be able to get out of the hole. Many don't know that the devil is speaking to their minds to try to tempt them to fall into sin. Warn others about it and teach others how to fight with my words. I give my children the power to overcome their enemies, but many do not use the weapons that I give them."

"Lord, tell me about those weapons!"

"They are prayer, the word of God, and resisting the devil in my name. People cannot fight the devil and win by themselves. They need my help, but many of my children don't believe in the existence of the devil. Many of my workers fall into this hole. They have been beaten by the devil and they didn't even know it."

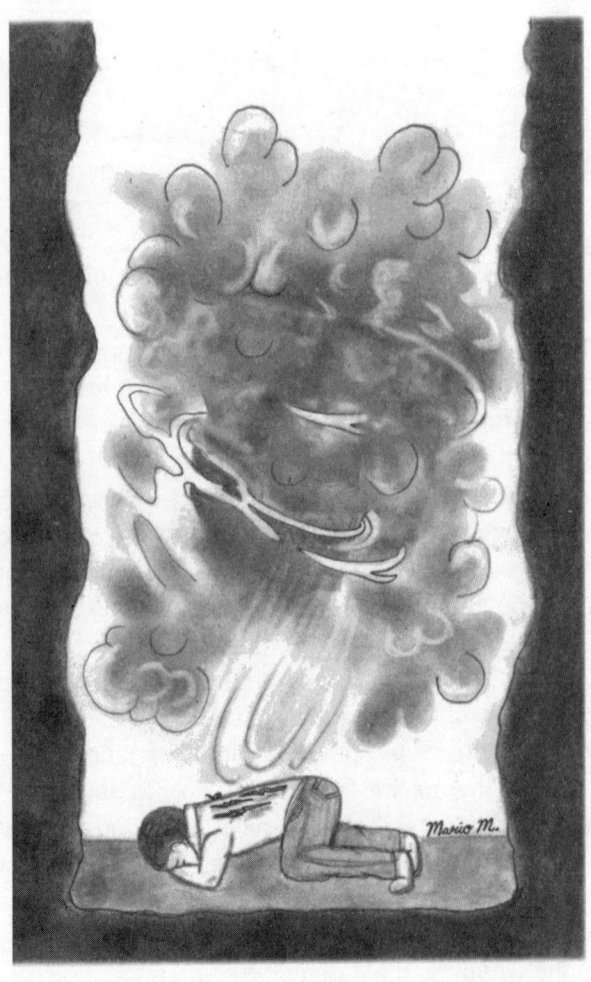

"My Lord, help me to help others who fall into these holes."

"My daughter, there are worse things than this. Come and follow me."

The next hole Jesus led her to had a demon in it who was telling one man to beat another man. The demon danced and laughed aloud when the man followed it's directions.

Jesus looked very sad. "My child, when someone attacks you, it's not just them doing it. Many times the devil speaks to people who don't have much respect for others and encourages them to start fighting. The man who has been attacked is a minister and the man who is beating the man is a leader of the church who causes lots of problems with other leaders. Do you see why many of my workers have a difficult time? Many people work for the devil. These people don't even know that they are being used by the devil to destroy the unity that I want for them."

"Lord, please help me to know what I should do."

"Pray for repentance, forgiveness, unity, and loving hearts. The harvest is plentiful but many are used by the devil and focus on attacking others. People who are fighting cannot focus on the harvest. They wound people and are wounded themselves. They can't obey my words. They don't go out to help others who need to hear the message of love, because they don't have love themselves."

The girl sang, "Lord Jesus, please help us to repent when we mistreat others with critical attitudes, words, and actions. Open our eyes to see and understand what's happening. Open our hearts to believe the word of God. Bless us with wisdom and knowledge to know what's happening in the spiritual world so we can fight the devil with your power. Please forgive those who destroy unity and peace. Help them to repent so they can create peace and plant the seeds of love. Help us to spread your message of love to the ends of the world. Lord Jesus, I love you. Help me to help others the way you want. Help me to spread your message of love to those who are in need of it. Help me to have the courage to speak the message you want me to spread. Let me love you, Lord Jesus. Help me to understand your love more. Help me to understand your heart so I can share it with others."

Jesus smiled. "My loving daughter, I am glad that you are listening. I am blessing you with this book to help leaders who are open to my words."

The girl smiled and danced for Jesus. "Lord, I will be open to your words."

17. Compassion

As they walked along, Jesus said, "Now, let's go and look for the lost sheep. Among them are many spiritual leaders who do not know me. They don't have my peace. I want you to keep speaking loudly so you can reach many leaders. I want them to hear my message of love and peace."

The girl sang, "Lord Jesus, help me to plant the seeds of your love and peace. Help them to seek you so they can meet you, understand your love, and have peace of mind."

"My loving daughter, I want you to keep walking with me and practicing silent prayer. Then you will be able to reach out to many people that you don't know through the books."

The girl answered, "Wow, Lord, you have many plans for me. Let me understand your plans and help me to obey you."

"To do that, you need to keep spending time with me. I will help you reach out to many people that you don't know. Keep writing what I give you."

"Lord, thank you for blessing this book. You blessed me through this book. I learned a lot about your heart. Help me to have your heart so I can do what you want me to do. I love you, Lord. Help me to love you even more."

Jesus' face was filled with joy. He looked more pleased than ever. The girl followed him as she sang with the birds. She doesn't know what the Lord will teach her next, but she knows that whatever he teaches her helps her love for him to grow.

"My loving daughter, come and follow me, I will help you to make disciples of all nations."

"Yes, Lord, I will follow you. Guide and direct me to do what you want me to do."

As they passed the mountain, the place they arrived at was full of tranquility and peace. The birds sang and wild flowers colored the valley. Then soon they arrived back in the valley covered with yellow dandelions.

The girl knew where she was. The mountain of distraction had taught her many lessons, especially that she needs to pray for the leaders, but she was glad that she was back at the beautiful flower bed. She felt immersed in the beauty.

She ran around the flower beds and exclaimed, "Wow, you brought me back to the place that I love the most."

"My loving daughter, I want you to enjoy the flowers in this valley. You will be able to work here until I will take you somewhere. I love you, daughter."

"I love you too! I have a question. You said that when I understand your heart, it will be sweet. Can you tell me more about what sweetness means? All the places we went were full of sad stories and I learned more about my weaknesses. There was nothing sweet about what I saw."

"My child, that's what I wanted you to see. Sweetness is my heart of compassion. I pray for those who have fallen in the holes. I want you to do the same. Your heart of compassion and prayers will help those who need wisdom to get out of the holes. If you don't understand what I mean, you will find answers in the future. At this moment, I want you to enjoy the flowers and continue your silent prayer."

The girl smiled. "You are going to let me enjoy the flowers. Thank you for teaching me what I need to be careful of and what to pray about."

Jesus said, "My loving daughter, I love you!"

The girl replied, "I love you, Lord Jesus, thank you for letting me rest here." The girl ran to the fields and started blowing the seeds into the air. She watched them and was amazed by their beauty. Wherever Jesus took the girl, she knew there were lessons for her to learn. She knew that's what Jesus wanted. Jesus' compassion is what he wanted her to have. However, she was glad that she was able to rest for now. Her joyful singing filled the valley. Jesus listened and smiled. He watched her with loving eyes. She felt love and now she knew about his compassion.

Journey With Jesus Four

The Power of the Gospel

Yong Hui V. McDonald

INTRODUCTION

Writing *Journey With Jesus Four , The Power of The Gospel* has blessed me. I was busy with studying, and the Lord stopped that temporarily and led me to write this in ten days. As with the other *Journey With Jesus* books, my writing was definitely inspired by the Lord.

I thank Jesus for all the lessons that he has taught me. I pray that the Lord will speak to and bless those who read this book. I give all the glory to my Lord Jesus.

Journey With Jesus Four, The Power of The Gospel

1. Beauty

The girl was singing with the birds in the valley full of dandelions.

Jesus gently tapped her shoulder and said, "My loving daughter, I need to show you some other places you haven't seen."

This time, the girl was delighted. She said, "Jesus, I am ready to go on another trip."

Jesus started walking and the girl followed him. She sang, "Jesus, you are the most beautiful person. You know what I need to learn. You teach me what others cannot teach me. I praise you and give you thanks for the peace and joy you have given me. Teach me how to love you more today. Teach me the lessons I need to learn from you."

Jesus looked at her with eyes filled with love and said, "My loving daughter, when you follow me with a contented heart, that makes me happy, and that's what you have now."

The girl looked at Jesus and smiled. "Lord, I used to think that you were demanding too much of me and my time. But now, I realize that you are my peace and joy, so I love to follow you."

"My daughter, this time I want you to write another book on *Journey With Jesus.*"

"I have lots of homework, but you are my first priority, and you will help me with homework later; so I will obey you."

"As long as you are walking with me, your book will continue."

Not long after they left the valley of flowers, they were walking in a valley filled with garbage, and there were many garbage cans overflowing there.

The girl said, "Lord, I've never seen anything like this in the mountains so close to the beautiful valley of flowers."

Jesus replied, "What you are seeing is a spiritual vision of people's hearts. I want you to see how people's hearts can be filled with garbage when they put worldly thoughts and worldly values in their hearts and live a sinful life. What you are seeing is what I see in some people who follow sinful desires and fall into sin."

"Lord Jesus, this is a stinky place."

"Yes, my daughter, and you will see how this place can turn into a beautiful garden."

"How?"

"When my children learn about me and my love, they can learn to love me, and this place can turn into a beautiful garden. Loving me will help people to cleanse their hearts. Now you know what you need to do. You have the responsibility to teach others how to love me."

"Oh, I get it. When people learn to love you, their hearts will be filled with beauty because you are beautiful."

Jesus smiled. "You understand the message. People need healing from loving the world, so they can create beauty with my love."

"Lord, how can people learn to love you?"

"They need to read the Bible and learn to pray to me and listen to the Holy Spirit and obey."

"It sounds simple, but why is it so hard for people to do that?"

"I need my workers to keep working on teaching people how to love me. That's why you are working on books about *Loving God*, which can help others."

The girl was delighted. "Lord, that's why you asked me to write books about *Loving God,* but it seems there aren't many people whose focus is on loving God."

"That's why I said the harvest is plentiful but the workers are few. That's why you need to work on training the leaders."

"Oh, Lord, I feel I haven't been doing well in that area. I need your wisdom to do that."

"I will train you to train others. You cannot teach others unless you first learn from me."

"Lord, I am ready to learn from you."

"To do that, you need to spend a lot of time praying in silence and listening to my voice."

2. Race Cars

The next place the Lord took her was a big auditorium and many race cars were waiting to start a race. The cars were waiting, but many of them didn't have air in their tires.

Only a few cars had tires that were ready to go.

The starting gun sounded, but only the few cars with inflated tires were able to move forward. People cheered for the cars that took off, but big sighs and disappointment filled the air for the cars that couldn't move forward. Some cars moved a little bit, but then stopped because their tires were flat.

The girl said, "Lord, why didn't these drivers see that they have flat tires?"

"This is a spiritual lesson. The drivers didn't check their tires because they were too busy with other things."

"But what about other people? Couldn't they have checked the tires and helped the drivers?"

"My loving daughter, this is the spiritual condition of many of my children; they are not prepared to follow me. Others who are not able to see the spiritual condition of people didn't see that the cars weren't ready."

"Jesus, what are you trying to teach me?"

"The flat tires signify that many have not relied on the Holy Spirit's leading. The Holy Spirit empowers people to move on with God's visions and dreams with special power. The Holy Spirit can empower them to do things that they need to do for God's kingdom. That's why I mentioned that people need to be filled with the Holy Spirit."

The girl opened her eyes wide. "Wow, Lord, I didn't know that the tires had something to do with the lessons of the Holy Spirit's filling. You are saying that being filled with the Holy Spirit is having the Holy Spirit's vision and dreams."

"That's right. Without the Holy Spirit's vision, people cannot move. There is a spiritual race that all people are in, but many do not know about it. Paul explained this race: 'Do you not know that in a race all the runners run, but only one gets the prize? Run in such a way as to get the prize. Everyone who competes in the game goes into strict training. They do it to get a crown that will not last; but we do it to get a crown that will last forever. Therefore, I do not run like a man running aimlessly; I do not fight like a man beating the air. No, I beat my body and make it my slave, so that after I have preached to others, I myself will not be disqualified for the prize.' (1 Corinthians 9:24-27) You are also in a race. You need to check your tires to make sure they are full of air. The Holy Spirit is the one who fills the tires with air, but when people don't rely on the Holy Spirit, their tires are flat."

"Lord, you are amazing. Now I understand the power of the Holy Spirit more. No wonder I couldn't do anything for you when I was running away from you and disobeying the Holy Spirit's calling to serve you."

As they watched, a few cars made it to the finish line, and people were cheering for them.

The girl said, "Lord, it seems there were so many who wanted to be in the race and thought they were prepared, but they couldn't even start. What can I do to make sure that I am at the line ready to start on time and then finish on time?"

"How much you love me and how much time you spend listening to my heart is up to you. That will determine whether you can start the race on time. You have been delaying the race. Haven't you noticed?"

"Lord, you saw it right. I don't know where to start. I need your wisdom to discern which area I need to work on. Sometimes I am not even sure if I am on the right path. I know you are patient with me."

"My loving daughter, do you realize that I asked you to visit 500 churches to talk about prison revival?"

"Lord, I need your guidance and direction to accomplish that."

"I will lead you. I will be with you. I will give you the words to say. I will open the doors for you. Until the time comes, keep listening to the Holy Spirit. You will know when you have to be at the starting line to run this race."

"Thank you so much for reminding me that you are the one who will guide and direct my path. Until then I am going to try to obey and do what you ask me to do."

"See, how many people were disappointed when all the racers couldn't take off in this race? Unfortunately, many of my children are not even able to start the race because they don't recognize that they need to rely on the Holy Spirit. That's what has been happening to you for a long time."

"Lord, you are right. I didn't know that the Holy Spirit could guide me to follow you, but now I know that I need to rely on the Holy Spirit in everything."

"Now you are getting it. I will help you join the race that I have called you for."

"Help me to do it to please you because I love you."

Jesus looked pleased. He gently touched the girl's head and said, "That's why I am asking you to follow me, so I can train you to be my disciple. Follow me; I have many things to show you."

3. A Lion and a Kitten

As they walked along, they heard the sound of a lion roaring. Soon they saw a lion chasing a little kitten. The kitten found a small hole and hid. The lion waited outside the hole for a while. Then, since the kitten wouldn't come out, the lion left. Jesus walked up to the hole and spread his hands out. The kitten jumped into his hands. Jesus patted the little kitten and turned to the girl and said, "My daughter, many people do not know about the spiritual world and they are scared. They are like this little kitten. But I can help them and rescue them. You can teach them about my power."

The girl thought it was almost like having a dream. "Lord, what happened to that lion? It was here and then disappeared."

The Lord said gently. "That's the devil scaring people. When people don't walk with me, the devil scares them and many people act like a little kitten. I have the power to overcome the enemy. That's the power I give to people so they don't have to be afraid. I want you to be in my hands always, so you can be safe. The devil attacks people and scares them with anxiety, fear, worry, and panic attacks, but you just rely on me. I will be your peace, joy, and confidence in times of trouble. Keep praying so you will be able to discern what's happening to you, so you can win your spiritual battle and teach others to win their battles."

"Lord, I thank you so much for your protection. I have peace when you are holding me. Hold me close to your heart so I can understand your power and not be afraid."

"My daughter, when you try to do my work, you will be attacked by the devil. When that happens, it's time for you to pray more, so you can have the Holy Spirit's power to win the battle and find peace. Then, you will be able to teach others how to find peace."

They continued on their walk, and they found a little boy

who was hiding in a small hole. Jesus stretched out his hands and the boy came out. Jesus held him in his arms and said, "Look and see."

The girl was surprised to see the little boy. He was one of her family members for whom she had been praying for God's protection. She was delighted to see him. "Lord, thank you for helping him."

"I have answered your prayers my daughter. You don't have to worry about him."

"Thank you, Lord Jesus, for answering my prayers. I want to rest in your hands also, so I won't be scared of anything."

"As long as you keep praying and relying on the Holy Spirit and obeying, you will be resting in my hands. Come, now, I have other things to show you."

4. A Valley of Death

When Jesus and the girl arrived at the next mountain, many people were lying on the ground as though they were dead. When the girl got close to them, she realized that some of them were alive. They were very thin, and it looked as though they were dying from starvation. It was a horrible sight.

A man on the ground said, "I am thirsty." The Lord walked up to him and said, "Those who are thirsty, come to me and drink." He then gave him a cup of water and gave him a Bible.

The man started reading the Bible, and then he gained his strength and got up and started preaching. "Repent, believe the good news. The Kingdom of God is near." At this, other people who were on the ground started getting up as though they had regained their strength.

Jesus turned to the girl. "My daughter, do you know what I am trying to teach you?"

"Yes, Lord, I need to preach the gospel to raise the dying people."

Jesus smiled and said, "Now you are getting it. Do you see why I am asking you to share what I have told you?"

"Yes, Lord. The word of God has life."

"I am the life, and my words give strength to those who are weak. Make opportunities to share my words of life whenever you can."

"Thank you, Lord Jesus, for your guidance. I will do it. Actually, when I meditate on the word of God, I can feel the presence of God more than ever. Is this what you mean when you say that we can have life?"

"Yes, you can have life and come alive as you get closer to me. The word of God has the power to raise the dying people."

"Thank you, Lord, for the lesson."

"My daughter, the word of God is offensive to many people; therefore, many are dying without my words of life. Many people in the world have not heard the gospel, so keep

working on your book project to help as many as possible, so they can hear the message of love and life that comes from me."

"I will do it, Lord, when you open the doors for me."

"I will open many doors for you in the future. I want you to be prepared. I want you to follow me, so I can teach you other things."

By the time they left that valley, many people had stood up and were reading the Bible. A revival started in that valley. People found God and life.

'Why were there all these starving people?' The girl wondered.

The Lord understood her thoughts. "My daughter, many people may have heard about God and me, but they really don't know who I am. My workers should go to places like this and preach to those who have not heard about me. That's what you should do with the books. Send the books to places where not many people reach out."

"Yes, Lord, I will do it to follow you."

"Follow me; I have something else to show you."

5. Bug Houses

After they left the valley, the next place they went to was a mountain with many beautiful trees. From afar, the trees looked healthy; but when they were close, the girl saw many little sick trees with white bug nests on the branches, and some of the trees were dying.

The girl said, "Lord, I thought this tree was healthy, but it is really a sick tree."

"Yes, this is a condition of many of my children. Many say that they are working for me, but they have not taken care of all their past wounds; and they have angry, unforgiving hearts and grudges."

"Lord, how can we get rid of all the wrong thoughts and

attitudes?"

"People first have to recognize that they need to come to me to experience healing, but many do not. Their sin is they don't understand that they need to come to me and ask for healing. When they seek my healing power, they will be freed from their unforgiving hearts."

"Can you tell me more about this?"

"It starts with repentance. Unforgiving hearts produce bug eggs of hate, and more negative feelings. If people don't take care of it, they will be sick and unable to produce good fruits. When people repent, they are destroying the bug nests, and they get well. Many need healing in their hearts, and I want you to teach them how to experience healing through my healing words."

"Lord, what else do I need to know to teach others?"

"The Word of God is alive, and when they obey, they

can experience healing. Bless and pray for those who mistreat you. Love your enemies. These are the words that give the guidance to experience healing."

"Lord, help me to obey you."

"I will show you more things."

6. Tree Planters

They passed the side of the mountain with many trees and found the other side of the mountain was bare. There was a nursery where people were taking care of little trees, and some were planting the trees on the mountains.

Jesus looked pleased and said, "These are my workers. They are planting the seed of the gospel in places where the good news has not been heard. I want you to do the same."

"Lord, help me to do what you are asking me to do."

"You are planting the seed of the gospel when you send books to prisoners and hurting people. Many of them have not heard the gospel of the good news."

The girl replied, "Lord, let me continue to do this work. I need help from many others to expand this ministry so we can plant the seed of the gospel more than before. I want at least twenty-eight million copies of books distributed to prisons and homeless shelters all over the world."

"My daughter, keep following the Holy Spirit and pray so the doors will be open. You cannot do it, but the Holy Spirit can do it."

"Thank you, Lord. Why did I have this idea of sending so many books?"

"I have given you that vision and dreams. I will send more people to help you do what I want you to do."

The girl danced with Jesus. This time she sang, "Lord, Jesus, I love you. Let me see a smile on your face when the seed of the gospel flies all over the world to plant the love of the gospel. Let me see others grow in love for you."

Jesus' face brightened with a smile. "I want you to keep praying. That's what you are supposed to do so others can get help. When you work with leaders, you will see more fruit. They are the ones who can help you plant the seed."

"How can I work with leaders?"

"I want you to keep praying, so you can find the leaders that have the same heart as you."

The girl said, "Lord, open the doors so I can meet the leaders that have your heart so I can work with them. I learned that many people are not interested in prison ministry."

"You will find those people who can work with you. I will send the workers along the way so they can help you. There are many workers that can work with you."

"Lord, show me what's happening with the books."

"I want you to let your eyes see what I see."

The girl noticed something in the air flying, and it was one of the books that were sent to prisoners in other countries.

She exclaimed. "Lord, the book is flying. I hope that it will land in a prison."

"That's where it is going, my daughter. What you do for my kingdom will not be forgotten by me. Only those who sacrifice will see the fruit. I know who they are."

"Lord, you are amazing! I am so encouraged by this. What else can you show me that is encouraging?"

Jesus looked into her eyes and said, "Look at me. I love you, and that should be enough."

The girl giggled with delight. She said, "Yes, Lord. Your love fills my empty heart, and what more can I ask from you? I am so full of love because of you."

"Look in the sky again," Jesus said.

This time the girl saw a cement bridge in the air that was not connected to anything. She was in awe and could not find a word to say.

Jesus said, "My loving daughter, I will be blessing you with many international bridges that will help you spread the gospel."

The girl asked, "Why isn't this bridge connected to anything?"

"I will put bridges where you can walk to others and share my love. I will help you connect to many people who you don't know. I will send people to help you because mission is my project. As you know, your book project is my project."

"Thank you, Lord, for all your help."

"My daughter, I will provide everything you need."

Then the girl saw a door opening, but in front of it was a ladder blocking the way.

Jesus said, "My daughter, there are many things that you need to put away before I open many doors for you. You don't need to worry about money for the book project. I will provide all the funds for your ministry."

She thought about the cost of plane tickets if she needed to go to many places.

The Lord knew her thoughts and showed her what was blocking her.

"The ladder is worry about money. I provide what my workers need. Isn't everything mine? Why do you worry?"

The girl smiled. "Lord, I will trust you. Whenever you have asked me to do something, you always have provided for me. You provided all my tuition for school, and you have shown me that your grace is sufficient for me."

Jesus said, "My daughter, you are getting tired. That's why you are worrying. I will carry you for a while. Rest in my arms."

The girl said, "We have been walking for a long time. My legs are getting tired. I want to rest."

Jesus carried her in his arms and the girl felt his love and care. Jesus knew what she needed.

"I take care of my workers, and I will help you rest. I will take you to the next place."

7. Two Trees

This time Jesus took the girl to a place where a woman had two small plants. One was healthier looking than the other. She put the healthy plant in a hole, then put the sickly plant on top of it. Soon, both plants died.

The girl couldn't believe what she saw and asked, "Lord, why did she do that? She buried one tree and killed it, and now, the other tree also died."

"Many of my workers are planting the trees not on fertile ground but on top of other trees."

"I don't understand. I need you to explain this."

"Many of my children are not growing because they rely on people rather than relying on me. They only rely on the leader and not on the Holy Spirit's leading in their lives."

"She just let two nice looking trees die."

"My daughter, that's why many leaders are dying," They have many small plants growing on top of them. They teach them to be followers. Then, when the leader dies, the followers also die."

"Jesus, why is it so hard to remember to rely on the Holy Spirit?"

"Many are not helping others to seek me. This is a problem with many leaders. They have started their own empire with the little strength they have. They cannot teach their people since they are not relying on me. This woman thought that if a little plant is planted on top of the healthy plant, it will grow more, but she doesn't realize that the strong plant will die because it is buried under the other plant, and the top plant cannot grow on top of another plant."

"Lord, this lesson is difficult for me. I need your help. Does this mean that leaders shouldn't be mentors to others?"

"People need to be encouraged to find me and seek me, not to seek other people. Being a good mentor is directing others to me. That's what's lacking in people who think they know what they are teaching. They gather people for themselves."

"I'm sorry, Jesus. That's what I have done for a long time. Help me not to make mistakes."

Jesus said, "Many people misunderstand when I say 'feed my lambs.' What that means is not to make others follow them to be fed, but to lead them so they can be fed by me."

"Jesus, teach me how to be a mentor to others, so I can direct them to you according to your will."

"Many of my workers who are tired of helping and some others are in this condition. They made disciples of themselves and not me. That's why I want you to be careful. Don't lead others to follow you but to follow me. That's what I am trying to teach you."

"Being a mentor brought you many people who loved to follow you, but you didn't encourage them to follow me. That's why you felt exhausted. You were doing my work with your own strength and wisdom."

The girl sighed. "Lord, thank you so much for reminding me that if people follow me instead of following you, there will be times I will feel exhausted because I cannot feed them. I need to help them to focus on you."

"When you feel you are exhausted spiritually, you have tried to feed others instead of teaching them to be fed by me. I want them to have the word of God in their heart. People cannot grow when they rely on other people to be fed."

"Lord, all these years, I put so much emphasis on leadership, and I complained because they didn't have what I needed to learn. Now, I realize what you are saying. I need to make sure that others are growing in the Lord and not focus on myself. I get it."

Jesus smiled. "That was one of the reasons why I asked you to tell others to look up to me. Keep relying on the Holy Spirit to learn how to help others to plant the trees in the right places. You cannot be a mentor to people with only your own strength. You have to start with prayer for yourself and others."

"Lord, with your help, I want to make sure that people will follow you. Help me to pray more. Help me to teach others to focus on you and the word of God."

"When others become a burden to you, remember to remind them to turn to the word of God and the Holy Spirit. I will help you, my loving daughter."

"Can you explain more about what it means to follow you?"

"Following me means understanding my deep, never ending love for all people. They rely on me to find love, comfort, encouragement, and strength. People, even spiritual leaders, cannot give that to anyone. That's why you need to help others to come to me and not to you."

"Wow, Lord, why didn't I learn this earlier. I used to think I am supposed to be a mentor to leaders, and I couldn't figure out why I had problems with some people. Now, I realize that I made lots of mistakes."

"When you are acting as a mentor, you may not realize that you try to get strength from others. That's the danger of being a leader. Paul's goal was to understand me, and I want you to do the same."

"Now, I know what you are trying to tell me. Help me to love you and follow you. That's the most important thing in my life."

"I will help you follow me."

8. A Net

As the girl and Jesus walked along the road, they saw a

group of evil looking demons hidden in the bushes. When a woman passed by, they threw a net over her. The demons laughed at her. The net around her was made of some kind of white webbing. The woman kept kicking and screaming, but the demons would not release her. Instead, they threw her on the bush and left. She kept kicking, but the net didn't break.

The girl said, "Help her, Lord!"

Jesus said sadly, "You are looking into a spiritual vision. This woman was hurt and felt trapped many times in her life, but she didn't let go of her resentment and kept asking 'why' instead of forgiving. She is trapped in sin."

"But, Lord, how can she be freed?"

"Lord, is there any way others can help her?"

"She has to make the decision to forgive. She put herself in the devil's trap."

"Lord, please help her to forgive."

Jesus looked at the girl with sad eyes. "This is the trap that she has been in for 25 years."

"Lord, is there anything that I can do to help her?"

"Pray for her, so she can learn to forgive. Prayer breaks the bondage."

The girl sat by the woman, who was still inside the net and still kicking. The girl prayed, "Forgive me, Lord. Please help people who don't repent, who cannot forgive, so that they can be freed from the trap of the devil. Help her to forgive, so she can come out of that trap. Don't let her die in there."

The next thing she heard was the woman praying, "Jesus, please help me. I will forgive everyone who hurt me. I have sinned against you. Please forgive me. I only focused on what others did to me and their sins rather than on forgiving them. Send angels to cut this trap so I can be freed. I am having difficulty breathing."

Then two angels came and cut the net with scissors. Soon, the woman put her face out of the net and sighed.

"I can finally breathe. Why did I stay there for so long?"

Jesus said to the girl, "Your prayer helped her, and when she heard your prayer, she realized that she needed to forgive. A lesson of forgiveness is very difficult for many people. I want you to remember this. An unforgiving spirit can choke you, and you will be captured in the trap. Keep praying so you will be a blessing, not just to those who are nice to you, but also to those who aren't nice to you."

The girl replied, "Yes, Lord. I will try to remember to forgive."

"I will help you. I will show you other things. Follow me."

9. Different Shoes

As they walked along, the girl became tired. So, she said, "Lord, somehow my legs are so tired that I am having a difficult time walking. May we rest for a while?"

The girl sat down and noticed that she was wearing a tennis shoe and a high heel. She couldn't believe it. "I didn't realize that I was wearing two different shoes. What happened?"

Jesus replied, "My daughter, high heels represent your own will. The tennis shoe represents my plan to lead you on a comfortable journey so you can follow me."

"Actually, at the beginning of this journey, I was wondering why you would want me to write another book when I am behind on homework. But this kind of thing happened last year, and you helped me to finish the book and all my homework. So, I didn't worry, but still I wonder why you give me so many assignments. What are you trying to teach me?"

Jesus smiled. "I know your heart. You are learning how to obey me. Do you remember when I asked you to give me your plans? You said you would. Until you can completely turn your plans over to me, you can't follow me. You have

been following me for a while, but this trip is another trip that you have not planned; so you want comfort more than walking with me. You wanted to play with flowers, but I had a plan to teach you spiritual lessons that you can share with others who don't know me."

"Lord, how can I always obey you and follow you?"

"You have to let go of your plans and understanding. Then you have to learn to wait to understand my heart. Then, when you understand my heart and what I want from you, I will have new shoes for you."

Jesus gave her a pair of shoes that fit her. She was jumping with joy and said, "These are just right for me. They're comfortable. I can follow you now."

The girl took Jesus' hand and followed him and started singing, "Lord Jesus, you know my heart more than anyone. I seem to have my own plans and I try to follow them, but that hinders my following you. Thank you for giving me a new pair

253

of shoes so that I may follow you. Help me to follow you and not be distracted by my own thoughts and understanding. Help me to know your plans for me, and help me to obey you."

Jesus turned to her and said, "Keep singing, my daughter, and keep praying. That will help you to focus your heart on me."

10. A Church Doorknob

The next place Jesus took her was a small church on a mountain. When they arrived, the girl noticed the doorknob was quite worn and had been smashed.

The girl said, "Lord Jesus, why does this church have a doorknob like this? It would be nice if they had a new one to make this church look beautiful."

Jesus said, "My daughter, this doorknob represents many of my workers who have been worn out."

"Please, tell me more about it."

"Their life has been a sacrifice for me. People heard the gospel when they entered this church. Everyone had to use the doorknob to enter it. Those who work for me are used like a doorknob for the door to the kingdom of God. Those who were persecuted for their faith while presenting the gospel paid the price. Because of their sacrifice, the church door was open."

"Lord, what is the significance of the smashed doorknob?"

"This doorknob represents many people who worked for me and in the process faced many opponents and suffered. That's what you are seeing. People who do not have respect for me, do not have respect for people who work for me. In fact, they become destructive to my workers."

"How can I avoid people like that?"

"You need to be praying to receive discernment to avoid

certain situations and people who would cause distractions or attacks."

"Let me have your discernment, so I can be effective for God's kingdom."

"Pray for discernment. Keep praying for the spiritual leaders who are going through lots of suffering from the devil's attacks and are worn out. Many are losing spiritual strength because they are not relying on me for strength. You need to recognize that when your strength is weak, you are beginning to wear out; and when that happens, you need to come to me and spend more time with me, so you can find strength."

"Thank you, Lord Jesus. You are amazing. There are times I felt so worn out, and I didn't realize I was focusing on distraction rather than focusing on you. Please help me, so I can walk with you always and avoid things that will distract me from building the kingdom of God."

"My daughter, many of my workers are worn out. Keep praying for them. I have called you to pray for others to be strengthened by the Holy Spirit."

"Lord, I am praying for all your servants who are working for you and sacrificing their lives for the kingdom of God. Heal their wounds and give them the Holy Spirit's strength."

"Keep praying, my daughter. Follow me, my loving daughter. I will show you more things that you need to learn."

11. A Whip

Jesus took the girl inside the church where a woman was kneeling in prayer at the altar. Standing behind her was a man with a whip who was whipping her feet, cursing, and saying things to hurt her. The woman's feet were bare, and blood started coming out of one foot. The woman didn't move or say anything but kept praying.

The girl asked, "Lord, what's happening here?"

Jesus' eyes were filled with tears. He said, "This is what's happening to many of my workers who try to build my kingdom. My workers need more prayers, so they can lead others to my kingdom. Many self-centered leaders are distracting my workers by attacking them and hurting them. The man who is whipping her is one of the leaders in this church. She is one of the spiritual leaders, and she is trying to obey my call to pray."

"But why is this man whipping the woman?"

"He thinks he is right and that he can attack spiritual leaders when he doesn't like what's going on."

"Why isn't she stopping him? She is bleeding."

"My daughter, you are seeing a spiritual vision. I want you to see what's happening when she prays. She is asking for angels to bring her God's protection."

Not long after that, angels appeared in the church, and one angel covered the man's eyes with black cloth. The man seemed to be confused. He was still waving the whip but was not able to hit the woman's feet.

Then another angel tied the man's hands behind him, and he couldn't use the whip on her any longer. Then the angel who had covered his eyes gagged him so he couldn't speak.

The girl said, "Wow, you are teaching me the power of prayer."

"Yes, my loving daughter, when you face problems, I want you to come to me and ask for help. Angels can help."

"Why did that woman have bare feet?"

"She understands my presence, and she is on holy ground. I asked her to take her shoes off. She was obeying what I asked her to do, and the man took advantage thinking that she couldn't defend herself because she was praying."

"Lord, I didn't realize how much suffering spiritual leaders are going through. Lord Jesus, I am sorry that I didn't pray for the leaders as much as I should have. Send the angels to help the spiritual leaders who need help. Thank you for helping me to know what's happening."

"You asked me why there is not much revival. This is one of the reasons. Many of my workers are attacked and hurting, so they don't have the time and energy to cultivate the ground and plant the seed of the gospel. They are distracted and worn out."

"Jesus, help me to do what I need to do, praying for leaders, cultivating and planting the seed of the gospel."

Jesus smiled. "I want you to avoid this kind of situation by praying for yourself, as well. You need to be aware that people who seem to work for me are hurting others as well. Keep praying, my daughter."

"Thank you for your teaching, Lord."

"I will show you other things."

12. Backpacks

As they walked along the mountain road, they saw an endless line of people walking through the valley. It looked almost like a refugee line. All of them carried different sizes of backpacks. The ones with small backpacks kept moving along at a good pace, but the ones with large, heavy backpacks had a difficult time walking and they were far behind.

The girl turned to Jesus and asked, "Lord, why are some carrying huge backpacks and some small ones?"

"These people are on the way to my Heavenly Father's home. What you see are people's spiritual journeys. Many cannot make it to my Father's home because they are carrying big, heavy loads. Some carry small backpacks because they traded in a big backpack for a lighter load."

"Jesus, how can people trade in their huge backpacks?"

"My loving daughter, do you remember my words?

'Come to me, all you who are weary and burdened, and I will give you rest. Take my yoke upon you and learn from me, for I am gentle and humble in heart, and you will find rest for your

souls. For my yoke is easy and my burden is light.' (Matthew 11:28-30) The burden is in the backpack. I will show you something."

Jesus took her to a roadside where many of Jesus' workers were distributing small backpacks in exchange for big, heavy backpacks.

They shouted, "Repent and believe in the good news of Jesus Christ. Jesus died on the cross to forgive your sins. Come and leave all your heavy backpacks at the feet of Jesus and receive a light backpack that Jesus prepared for you. Have a humble heart. You have to carry a small backpack in order to get to the heavenly Father's kingdom. Jesus is coming soon. Believe the good news."

A man who had a huge backpack was on his knees and cried, "God, I ask for your forgiveness. Jesus, come into my life and take away my entire burden. I will follow you."

A man put his heavy backpack down and received a small one which contained a Bible. He started reading the Bible as he walked along with others who carried light backpacks. He said, "Thank you, Lord, for saving me. Thank you for taking away my burden of sin and giving me the road map to get to my heavenly Father's kingdom."

Jesus turned to the girl with his face full of joy. "Did you see what happened? My workers are helping people who are tired of their journey because of their big backpacks. Now, they can follow me on the way to my Father's home."

"It's amazing what you do. Let me carry a small backpack, so I don't get distracted on my journey."

"You are trying. I know you have many distractions on your journey, but I will help you discern how to spend your time, so you can pray more and focus your heart on me rather than on worldly things. Then, you will be able to do what I want you to do."

"Lord, what's in the big backpacks?"

"People's ideas, sinful desires, and habits of the world fill the big backpacks. Those who love themselves and love the world more than they love me are carrying the heavy backpacks. Because of those who preach the gospel, there are people who can trade a heavy backpack for a light backpack."

The girl was amazed. "Lord, now I understand why I need to preach the gospel more than before. People can exchange their heavy burden for the lighter burden that you give us. No wonder people with lighter burdens have happy faces."

"Now, my daughter, you see why you need to keep preaching, so others can walk with me."

"Let me preach for you, Lord. I am here for you. Let me work for you."

"My daughter, I'm pleased with your obedience."

"I am sorry, Lord, for the way I was. Help me stay on the right path."

"Come, follow me. I will show you other things."

13. Metal Backpack

As they walked along the road with people who had Jesus' light backpacks, the girl saw a crying woman sitting on the side of the road. She had a big black backpack, different from the others which were white.

When she got close, the girl noticed that the woman's backpack was made of metal, and it was obvious that she couldn't even get up because it was so heavy. The woman tried to take off the backpack, but it was so tightly fastened that she couldn't remove it.

The girl asked, "Lord, I didn't know that there were metal backpacks. I thought she received a light backpack a while back. Why is she wearing this heavy, black metal backpack now?"

"My daughter, you have seen it right. She did receive a light one, but later she traded for this one."

"Jesus, what happened to her?"

"My child, she is one of my workers. She was doing fine

at first with the light backpack. She began to share the gospel message to help others. The problem started when she began to think she was doing it with her own power. She was deceived into thinking that she had special gifts and power. The spirit of pride deceived her, and she thought that she could use her gifts and skill to manipulate people to get attention. What she didn't realize is that all things come from me, her life and even her skills, but she was using them for her own satisfaction. She didn't give glory to me for what I did."

"Lord, I am sorry. It's so easy to fall into a trap of pride, and I know I have done that as well."

"I don't want her to use my power for her own glory. People who work for themselves elevate themselves when it was the Holy Spirit who did all the work. For their own good, I would rather they not be effective."

"Lord, what does she need to do to be freed from that heavy burden?"

"Everything is possible. Only if she repents will she be freed."

"Jesus, please help her to repent."

The woman was praying and asking God to forgive her. She started wiggling one of her arms out of the backpack straps.

Jesus said, "She finally recognized that repenting is the only key to freeing herself from the sin of pride."

The woman started crying out loud and said, "Lord, forgive me. I went the wrong way. Have mercy on me and save me from this heavy bag." She prayed more and tried to wiggle out slowly, but she was still stuck.

The girl asked, "What is it, Lord? What's slowing her down from being released from it?"

"She still needs a lot of healing in the areas where she gave herself credit. She still needs to repent in some areas, so she won't go back to having that backpack. Sometimes, healing takes time. When her heart is purified she will be able to get out of that harness."

The woman continued to pray and was slowly getting out of the backpack's straps. Then a man came along and gave her a light backpack. She put it on, and she started working. Her face was filled with joy and she said, "Lord, thank you for your forgiveness."

She started reading the Bible as she walked toward the heavenly Father's house.

Jesus' face shined. "Everyone who repents will receive a light backpack and can follow me."

14. Black Spots

As they walked along with many people who carried light backpacks, the girl noticed a woman who had black spots on her skin all over her body. Her eyes were filled with sadness, and she occasionally sighed and looked up to the sky as if she were lost.

The girl asked, "Jesus, why does this woman have spots all over her skin?"

"You are looking at her spiritual condition. This woman was hurt while she was growing up, so she thinks everyone will hurt her eventually. She can't trust others, so she attacks others and hurts them. She is in so much pain that she can't feel others' pain."

"How can she be healed from her past wounds?"

"My daughter, I want you to know that there are many people who are hurting like her. They need healing, and my words can heal them. The problem with this woman is that she knows the Bible, but she has not opened her heart to it."

"Lord, how can she accept the word of God, so she can experience healing?"

"When people pray more, they can recognize my presence, and the Holy Spirit will give them wisdom to

understand the Bible so they can be healed. Those who spend time with me will experience healing and will understand the word of God is alive."

"Lord, I see you are talking about silent prayer."

"Yes, when people don't understand the Bible, they need to pray for wisdom. Silent prayer helps them to understand my presence. But many people don't come to my presence, and they try to understand the Bible with their own wisdom. The Holy Spirit told her to pray more, and He would lead her to silent prayer. If she prays and listens to my voice of love and encouragement, she will be healed."

The woman with spots looked very tired. She knelt down on the ground and started to pray. "Lord, heal my skin. Others said that they heard your voice. Let me hear your loving voice." The woman sat in silence for a while and waited to hear from the Lord.

Jesus went to the woman and put his hands on her head and said, "My daughter, I know your pain. I love you. Be healed."

The woman cried. "Jesus, thank you for your love. I hurt others because they didn't love me. Now, that's not important to me anymore. Your love is what I needed. I forgive everyone who hurt me. Please forgive me for hurting others. Heal my wounds."

As she sat praying and crying, the spots on her face started disappearing. Then all her skin was healed, there were no scars and her face was bright. When she realized that all her skin was cured, she jumped with joy and started telling others how Jesus had healed her. She joined others and started walking toward the heavenly Father's home.

The girl exclaimed. "Jesus, your love and power are amazing."

"My child, that's only one event. Many are being healed with my word of life all over the world. Many miracles are happening."

"Lord, I believe what you are saying."
"Come and follow me, my loving daughter."

15. Overdone Cookies

As they walked along, a group of people who carried light backpacks said that they were getting hungry, and they started a fire and put cookie dough on a pan on the fire.

They sat by the fire and were busy talking. By the time that they checked, the cookies were burning. They took them off the fire quickly, but it was too late. They were all burnt and black. They didn't have any more ingredients to make more cookies, so they got up and started walking.

Jesus looked at the girl and sighed. "My daughter, this has a spiritual lesson. Many people talk about the gospel in church, and they say that they want to spread the gospel, but they only talk and do nothing. As with those burnt cookies, time is running out. The time is short. The time is coming when they won't have time to spread the gospel. Many are busy doing what they want to do and waste time, but they

have no heart to spread the gospel. Many don't know that people are walking towards burning hell and need to hear the message of salvation and be warned. My people need to follow my word and make disciples of all nations."

"Lord, Jesus, please forgive me. That's where I was for a long time."

"You need to keep preaching the gospel and encourage others to do the same. I want the gospel message to be preached, not only in church but everywhere. I need more people to do the mission work of reaching out to people who don't know me."

"Lord, help me to do what you want me to do."

"I want you to help the leaders who are called to the ministry."

"Thank you, Lord. Help me to obey you."

"I will help you."

16. Salt Shaker

Jesus took her to a restaurant, and when they sat at the table, the Salt Shaker didn't have any salt in it, but steam was coming out of it.

The girl asked, "Lord, why doesn't this Salt Shaker have any salt?"

Jesus looked at her sadly. "My daughter, this Salt Shaker represents my children's spiritual condition. I told my children to be the salt and light of the world, but many are not paying attention to what I have said."

The girl looked at the other tables and saw they all had empty Salt Shakers with steam coming out of the holes. "Jesus, why don't all the other Salt Shakers on the tables have salt?"

"This is a condition of many churches. They need to be the salt and light for the world, but they don't have anything to give to the world or any way to show others that they are the light of the world."

"Why is steam coming out of the Salt Shakers when there is nothing in them?"

"My child, the steam represents people's talk. People talk about the gospel message and how good it is, but they are not sharing it with the world."

"Lord, how can I be the salt of the world?"

"Preach the gospel. You are sending books to prisons and to hurting people. That is planting the seed of the gospel. I also want you to preach to the world about my message of love. Many are only looking out for their own interests and do not have any concern for saving souls. I want you to move forward with the visions I have given you and reach out to those who are hungry for the word and hungry for the message of hope and salvation."

"Lord, help me to do it!"

"You need to know that many people are dying now and will go to eternal, burning hell and suffer. I see their tears now. Many of my children are seeing what I am seeing, but they are not working for me. Instead, they are working for the flesh and working for themselves. They can't see the tears of suffering people."

"What shall I do?"

"I called you to warn people who are satisfied with where they are and don't have any desire to follow me. They have forgotten what's important in life. What good is it if you gain the whole world but lose your soul? That's the condition of many people."

The girl became sad. "That was my condition for a long time. How can I have love for the lost people like you do?"

"My daughter, you have started understanding my heart. I will share more with you as you walk with me. Now, just do what you need to do every day for my glory and walk with me and listen to me. Obey the Holy Spirit's leading. That's all I ask of you."

"Thank you Jesus. I want to know your heart, and I want to have your heart."

"My loving daughter, your words make me happy. Follow me. I need to show you other places."

17. Pumpkins

This time the Lord took the girl to a nice neighborhood where the lawns were well manicured. One house had many pumpkins on top of the grass. It seemed like the pumpkins had been on top of the grass for such a long time that some of them had rotted and the grass had died.

The girl thought that was odd. "Jesus, why is this lawn covered with pumpkins and all the grass is dead?"

"My daughter, it tells about many of my children's spiritual conditions. Their hearts are so heavy with love of the world and worries and concerns of this world that they cannot grow, but they are dying. People who don't follow me and live a life of sin are pressed down with heavy burdens. They wander around in the Valley of Death, and then they eventually die."

"What do these pumpkins represent?"

"They represent their love for the world. Anyone who doesn't love me loves the world."

"How can we be healthy and remove the heavy burden of sin? It seems impossible for the grass to move the pumpkins."

"Everything is possible with God. The Holy Spirit will help them. The Holy Spirit can help everyone who repents. Tell others to repent and turn their hearts to me. If they repent, then I will give them the Holy Spirit to remove all their burdens and help them live a holy life that will make them grow."

"Thank you, Lord, for the lesson. Please help me not to fall into the sin of the flesh and loving the world more than loving you. Help me to repent and walk with you. Purify me so I can love you with all my heart, mind, soul, and strength. I am learning that I cannot do it on my own and I need your help on this."

Jesus smiled at her. "I know that. I will help you. The Holy Spirit will help you. My Father will help you. Keep walking with me, and then you will see what is right and wrong. Now, let's go. It's time to show you something else."

18. Flowers

This time Jesus took her to a desert where the sun was beating down hard. There was nothing but sand. The girl missed the mountains, trees and the shade the trees provided. After a while, the girl saw a thin tree. At first, she thought the tree was dead since there was no water in the desert. When she walked closer to the tree, she saw that it wasn't dead. It just looked like it was dead, but she saw that a yellow flower bloomed on it.

The girl exclaimed, "Jesus, I thought this tree was dead, but I see a beautiful flower. I can't believe it."

"My daughter, this flower has a lesson for you. I have a bigger task for you reaching out to more people than you have been."

"Jesus, what are you talking about? You already have given me enough work to do."

"I will be opening more doors for you."

"What are you telling me now? Why are you showing me this flower?"

"Remember this. You will see flowers blooming in places where you never expected to see them."

"Lord, you are amazing. I pray that you will let your will be done in my life."

"My daughter, I will be answering your prayer."

"Which one are you talking about? I have been asking you for many things."

"Your prayer for growth of the prison ministry book project. Your books will go to places that you never guessed or imagined. I will send them out into the world to reach out to people who are hungry for my loving words. You will be blessed through it."

"Lord, you already have blessed me, and I am so happy that you have given me this desire to share the books with prisoners."

"I will be blessing you more than you can ever think or imagine. It will be more than prisoners. I will send them to those who have the desire to know me. The Holy Spirit will lead you. Can you tell that my words bring you strength, courage and encouragement?"

"Lord, you are right. You gave me this project when I was spiritually tired of my study and other concerns, but you brought me out of the pit when I was thinking I needed rest."

"You are in my arms, my daughter. I am reviving you."

"Thank you, Lord. I felt like I was spiritually dying. I thought maybe you were asking me to rest more. I found rest in you after you asked me to write this book. I thank you for leading me to look up to you so I can be revived. Now, I have more strength to go on."

"I knew you were weighed down with many assignments and you needed rest. I am going to lead you to see more flowers in the desert. Come follow me."

"How can I see many flowers in this desert?" the girl wondered. Then something unexpected happened. There was a big garden city in the desert. "How can a desert have a garden like this?" The girl was amazed. Inside the garden, there were many dead looking trees that had many beautiful blossoms, not just one but many blossoms. They were beautiful. A few people gave water to the trees and moved fast to take care of the trees."

"Lord, I cannot believe this."

"Those who believe in me and obey can do more than what I have done. These people who are taking care of the flowers are those who have seen miracles because of their faith."

"Even though there are only a few people here, this garden is big and there are many flowers blooming on the trees."

Jesus said, "See what I have told you. There are many missionaries who sacrifice their lives in places like this desert. They are my faithful servants who dig holes to have water for thirsty people, tend the sick, feed the hungry and preach the gospel to save their souls. Do you understand why there are many flowers? It's because of my sons and daughters who

sacrificed their lives and went to places not many people want to go, and they focused on saving dying souls."

"My Lord, why are there only a few people?"

"Many are not willing to go to places where there are deserts, scorpions and snakes, where they can be hurt and even die. But they are my faithful workers. What they are doing is glorifying me and saving dying souls. The flowers you saw represent those who have been saved and found new life in me. You can see the miracles with the book project."

"Wow, Lord, you are amazing. I want to have a heart like these people who have the faith and courage and vision to obey what you are asking them to do."

"My daughter, do what you need to do and care for the prisoners with books. And at the end, you will see the fruit in the future even though you may not see it in this life."

"Lord, I already have received more than I have given. You blessed me so much with the book project that I could die today and I would be satisfied."

"Now, my daughter, you don't know the plans that I have for you. Your vision is always too small, and I will send people who have bigger visions than you, so you can broaden your vision to reach out to more people than you have imagined."

"Lord, send me people with your visions and help me to see how the Holy Spirit can lead this book project to reach out to hurting people."

"My daughter, I will share my heart with you as I walk along with you. If I tell you now, you will not believe it, so I will share only a little with you now. Follow me."

The girl followed Jesus, singing and knowing that Jesus will always be with her as long as she holds his hand. It was a sweet walk with Jesus. Jesus' face shined full of love. The girl's face shined as she looked at his face.

"Jesus, your love, your amazing love, I can't express it with words. If I die while talking about your love, I will still be happy. Teach me about your love."

Jesus sang to her. "My daughter, your love is more beautiful than the flowers in the field. I will teach you my love. Read the Bible. Read 1 Corinthians 13 to understand my love for you."

The girl opened the Bible and read it. She started meditating on the Word. "If I speak in the tongues of men and of angels, but have not love, I am only a resounding gong or a clanging cymbal. If I have the gift of prophecy and can fathom all mysteries and all knowledge, and if I have a faith that can move mountains, but have not love, I am nothing. If I give all I possess to the poor and surrender my body to the flames, but have not love, I gain nothing. Love is patient, love is kind. It does not envy, it does not boast, it is not proud. It is not rude, it is not self-seeking, it is not easily angered, it keeps no record of wrongs. Love does not delight in evil but rejoices with the truth. It always protects, always trusts, always hopes, always perseveres." (1 Corinthians 13:1-7)

19. The Gown

As they walked along, the girl asked, "Lord, before I followed you to serve you, I had listened to over 5,000 sermons, but still I didn't give my life completely to you and did whatever I wanted to do. As I walked with you, I began to understand my sin and your love for the lost people, so I finally decided to follow you. I don't know why other people's sermons didn't bring transformation, but as I walked with you, I had transformation. When I think about that, I don't know if preaching is that significant. I don't even want to preach. I want to do things to change other people's hearts. How can I be anointed so that when I preach, the Holy Spirit will come down the way He did when Peter preached?"

"You asked a good question. If you obey and follow the Holy Spirit's leading, you will see miracles like Peter has done. The most important thing you need to know is this: Everything you do for my kingdom is not done by your own power but by the Holy Spirit. Also, what you need to focus on is not the result but whether you have obeyed the Holy Spirit. Not all the people who heard Paul and Peter believed in me. Only those who had open minds accepted the gospel message. I have something that I am preparing for you."

"What is it?"

"I am going to give it to you when you are ready." Jesus' hands were behind his back as though he were holding something.

"What do I need to get ready?"

"When you work for me, this is a very important lesson that you need to learn. You told me that five thousand sermons you heard didn't bring you transformation in your heart. You were also disappointed by my workers because of it."

"Yes, I was disappointed, and that's one of the reasons why I didn't want to preach. But now I know all I have to focus on is to obey the Holy Spirit. The reason I was disappointed was because I misunderstood about the role of spiritual leaders. Five thousand sermons helped me to get to know God, but my transformation didn't come from them. All the transformation of my heart happened when you started speaking to me and when I recognized your love and the power of the Holy Spirit."

"My daughter, you are getting ready to receive what I have prepared for you. When you believe that the Holy Spirit is doing all the work and obey, you will not depend on your wisdom. You don't have the power to transform other people, but the Holy Spirit can do it. If you know this, then you will not try to give yourself glory which belongs to me."

"Lord, now I have more respect for pastors, missionaries and other spiritual leaders. They know that they don't have the power to transform people's hearts. They have relied on the Holy Spirit, and they obeyed their call. Because of them, the gospel message is being spread throughout the world. Thank you for helping me to recognize this."

"I am glad that you have more respect for people who work for me. They are the ones who are working with the Holy Spirit. Now, I am going to give you what I have prepared."

The Lord showed her a white gown made from silk. "This gown is given to those who understand that people's transformation doesn't come from them."

Jesus put the gown on her.

"You can have this because you recognize that all the work you do is not done by your power but by the Holy Spirit's power. If you don't recognize it, you will start giving yourself credit and giving yourself glory. Then you will fall."

The girl was filled with joy. "Jesus, you are teaching me about humility, and that's your grace. I don't have anything, but everything is yours. The reason I see many miracles is because the Holy Spirit is opening people's hearts. I give you glory for all the things you have done in my ministry."

"My loving daughter, I am glad that you have learned from me. You have been walking with me for a while, so you are tired. I will take you to the flower valley so you can rest."

"Really, I would like to rest for a while."

The girl followed Jesus on a sunny day. Before long, they had reached the valley of flowers. The girl ran to the flowerbed for a while and then blew on the dandelions and watched a butterfly.

She thought about what the Lord had said. He told her to visit 500 churches to talk about prison revival, but if she plays in the flowerbed, she doesn't think she will be able to visit that many churches. The girl turned to Jesus and said, "Lord, you told me that if I follow you, you will give me a light backpack. But it seems the bag you gave me is a heavy one."

Jesus understood her thought and said, "The one you feel is a heavy backpack is called a love backpack. That is actually my backpack."

"You took me here and let me rest; but if I just play in the flowerbed, how can I visit that many churches?"

"My child, you don't need to worry about that. When you try to do my work, you won't be doing it. I will be doing it. All you have to do is to obey the Holy Spirit's voice every day, and then the Spirit will lead you to where I want you to go. Then you will be able to do what I want you to do."

"You told me that what I am carrying is a love backpack. Please tell me more about it."

"My beloved daughter, people that I have called to serve me carry a heavy love backpack that I gave them. People who carry this understand my heart and they have this urgency to save the lost people who are in torment. I help those who carry my love backpack. Those who cry and are praying for the lost are carrying it. Those who shed tears and cry out to me because they feel the pain of others carry it. When you spend more time in silent prayer, you will understand my love backpack. You have been walking with me for a long time, and you are tired, so it's time to rest. As you walk with me, you will understand this more, and you will also learn that you won't be carrying it with your strength. At this point, you just need to understand my love and walk with me so you can learn to love me."

With his eyes full of love, Jesus watched the girl. Jesus wouldn't say anything so the girl started singing, "Lord Jesus, I love you. I want to love you more."

The valley was filled with the laughter of the girl and Jesus. A gentle breeze touched the girl's hair, and she knew whenever she was with Jesus, there would be only love and joy.

Appendices

An Invitation

Do you have an empty heart that doesn't seem to be filled by anyone or anything? God can fill your empty heart with His love and forgiveness. Do you feel your life has no meaning, no direction, no purpose, and you don't know where to turn to find the answers? It's time to turn to God. That's the only way you will understand the meaning and the purpose of your life. You will find direction that will lead you to fulfillment and joy. Is your heart broken and hurting, and you don't know how to experience healing?

Until we meet Christ in our hearts, we cannot find the peace and healing that God can provide. Jesus can help heal your broken heart. If you don't have a relationship with Christ, this is an opportunity for you to accept Jesus into your heart so you can be saved, and find peace and healing from God. Here is a prayer if you are ready to accept Jesus:

"Dear Jesus, I surrender my life and everything to you. I give you all my pain, fear, regret, resentment, anger, worry, and concerns that overwhelm me. I am a sinner. I need your forgiveness. Please come into my heart and my life and forgive all my sins. I believe that you died for my sins and that you have plans for my life. Please heal my broken heart and bless me with your peace and joy. Help me to cleanse my life, so I can live a godly life. Help me to understand your plans for my life and help me to obey you. Fill me with the Holy Spirit, and guide me so I can follow your way. I pray this in Jesus' name. Amen."

Transformation Project Prison Ministry (TPPM)
(변화 프로젝트 교도소 문서 선교)

The Transformation Project Prison Ministry, a 501(c)(3) non-profit organization, produces and publishes books and DVDs and distributes them to prisons, jails, and homeless shelters nationwide. TPPM produces *Maximum Saints* books and DVDs transformation stories of inmates at Adams County Detention Facility, in Brighton, Colorado. Your donation to TPPM is 100% tax deductible. TPPM has distributed over 200,000 books and DVDs free of charge. If you would like to be a partner in this very important mission of reaching out to prisoners and homeless people or want to know more about this project, please visit online at: www.tppmonline.org and you can donate on line or you can write a check addressed to:

Transformation Project Prison Ministry
P.O. Box 220
Brighton, CO 80601

Website: www.tppmonline.org
Facebook: http://tinyurl.com/yhhcp5g
Email: tppm.ministry@gmail.com

TPPM is established in South Korea.
Contact: Rev. Lee Born, Director of TPPM
이본 목사
변화 프로젝트 교도소 문서 선교 지부장
Website: http//blog.daum.net/hanulmoon24

Prison Ministry Transformation Project (PMTP)
(교정선교 변화 프로젝트, South Korea)

PMTP reaches out to prisoners, homeless people, hospital patients, and people who have been deported from America to South Korea. PMTP distributes Christian books in prisons. For information about how to support this ministry, please contact:

Reverend Lee Born
Inchon-city, Namdong-gu, Guwol 3-dong, 1888-15
Republic of Korea, Zip code: 405-840
이 본 목사, 교정선교 변화 프로젝트 회장
인천시 남동구 구월3동 1388-15,
우편번호 405-840
Cell: 010-2210-2504, Office: 070-8278-2504
Email: leeborn777@hanmail.net
Website: http//blog.daum.net/hanulmoon24
Website: http//blog.daum.net/leeborn777

Veterans Twofish Foundation (VTF)

Veterans Twofish Foundation, a 501(c)(3), non-profit organization, produces, publishes, and distributes stories of veterans and veterans' families. They provide emotional and spiritual support and encouragement to veterans and their families through chaplain's services. Your donation is 100% tax deductible. If you would like to be a partner in this very important mission of reaching out to veterans, or want to know more about this project, please visit them online at: www. veteranstwofish.org.

Veterans Twofish Foundation
P.O. Box 220
Brighton, CO 80601

About The Author

Yong Hui V. McDonald, also known as Vescinda McDonald, is a United Methodist minister, chaplain at Adams County Detention Facility (ACDF) in Brighton, Colorado. She is a certified American Correctional Chaplain, spiritual director and on-call hospital chaplain.

She is the founder of the following:
- Transformation Project Prison Ministry (TPPM), a 501 (c)(3) non-profit, in 2005. TPPM produces Maximum Saints books and DVDs of ACDF saints stories of transformation and they are distributed freely to prisons, and homeless shelters.
- GriefPathway Ventures LLC, in 2010, to produce books, DVDs, and audio books to help others to process grief and healing.
- Veterans Twofish Foundation, a 501(c)(3) non-profit, in 2011, to reach out to produce books written by veterans and veterans' families to reach out to other veterans and their families.

Education:
- Multnomah University, B.A.B.E. (1980~1984)
- Iliff School of Theology, Master of Divinity (1999~2002)
- Asbury Theological Seminary student (2013-present)

Books and Audio Books by Yong Hui:
- *Journey With Jesus, Visions, Dreams, Meditations & Reflections*
- *Dancing In The Sky, A Story of Hope for Grieving Hearts*
- *Twisted Logic, The Shadow of Suicide*
- *Twisted Logic, The Window of Depression*
- *Dreams & Interpretations, Healing from Nightmares*

- *I Was The Mountain, In Search of Faith & Revival*
- *The Ultimate Parenting Guide, How to Enjoy Peaceful Parenting and Joyful Children*
- *Prisoners Victory Parade, Extraordinary Stories of Maximum Saints & Former Prisoners*
- *Four Voices, How They Affect Our Mind: How to Overcome Self-Destructive Voices and Hear the Nurturing Voice of God*
- *Tornadoes, Grief, Loss, Trauma, and PTSD: Tornadoes, Lessons and Teachings—The TLT Model for Healing*
- *Prayer and Meditations, 12 Prayer Projects for Spiritual Growth and Healing*
- *Invisible Counselor, Amazing Stories of the Holy Spirit*
- *Tornadoes of Spiritual Warfare, How to Recognize & Defend Yourself From Negative Forces*
- *Tornadoes of Accidents, Finding Peace in Tragic Accidents*
- *Lost But Not Forgotten, Life Behind Prison Walls*
- *Loving God, 100 Daily Meditations and Prayers*
- *Journey With Jesus Two, Silent Prayer and Meditation*
- *Journey With Jesus Three, How to Avoid the Pitfalls of Spiritual Leadership*
- *Loving God Volume 2, 100 Daily Meditations and Prayers*
- *Women Who Lead, Stories about Women Who Are Making A Difference*
- *Loving God Volume 3, 100 Daily Meditations and Prayers*

- *Journey With Jesus Four, The Power of the Gospel*
- Complied and published *Tornadoes of War, Inspirational Stories of Veterans and Veteran's Families* under the Veterans Twofish Foundation.
- Compiled and published five *Maximum Saints* books under the Transformation Project Prison Ministry.

DVDs:
- *Dancing In The Sky, Mismatched Shoes*
- *Tears of The Dragonfly, Suicide and Suicide Prevention*

Books Translated into Spanish:
- *Twisted Logic, The Shadow of Suicide*
- *Journey With Jesus, Visions, Dreams, Meditations and Reflections*
- *Maximum Saints Forgive*

Books Translated into Korean (한국어로 번역된 책들):
- 『예수님과 걷는 길, 비전, 꿈, 묵상과 회상』 (*Journey With Jesus, Visions, Dreams, Meditations & Reflections*)
- 『치유, 사랑하는 이들을 잃은 사람들을 위하여』 (*Dancing In The Sky, A Story of Hope for Grieving Hearts)*
- 『꿈과 해석, 악몽으로부터 치유를 위하여』 (*Dreams & Interpretations, Healing from Nightmares)*

- 『나는 산이었다, 믿음과 영적 부흥을 찾아서』
  (*I Was The Mountain, In Search of Faith & Revival*)
- 『하나님의 치유를 구하라, 자살의 돌풍에서 치유를 위하여』 (*Twisted Logic, The Shadow of Suicide*)
- 『승리의 행진, 미국 교도소와 문서 선교 회상록』
  (*Prisoners Victory Parade, Extraordinary Stories of Maximum Saints & Former Prisoners*)
- 『네가지 음성, 악한 음성을 저지하고 하나님의 음성을 듣는 영적 훈련』 (Four *Voices, How They Affect Our Mind*)
- 『하나님 사랑합니다, 100일 묵상과 기도』 (*Loving God, 100 Daily Meditations and Prayers*)
- 『영적 전쟁에서의 승리의 길』 (*Tornadoes of Spiritual Warfare, How to Recognize & Defend Yourself From Negative Forces*)
- 『예수님과 걷는 길 2편, 침묵기도와 묵상』 (*Journey With Jesus Two, Silent Prayer and Meditation*)
- 『우울증과 영적 치유의 길』
  (*Twisted Logic, The Window of Depression*)
- 『예수님과 걷는 길 3편, 영적인 여정에서 위험한 함정들』
  (*Journey With Jesus Three, How to Avoid the Pitfalls of Spiritual Leadership*)
- 『하나님 사랑합니다 2편, 100일 묵상과 기도』 (*Loving God Volume 2, 100 Daily Meditations & Prayers*)
- 『자녀들의 영적 성장을 위한 지침서』
  (*The Ultimate Parenting Guide*)
- 『멀고도 험한 길의 회상집, 미 육군 유격대 리키의 이야기』 (*The Long Hard Road, U.S. Army Ranger Ricky's*

Story with Reflections) *리키 라마와 이영희 지음 (Ricky Lamar and Yong Hui V. McDonald)*

- 『전쟁의 폭풍속에서, 퇴역 군인들과 그 가족들의 회상록』 (*Tornadoes of War, Inspirational Stories of Veterans and Veteran's Families*)

- 『용서의 기쁨』 (*Maximum Saints Forgive*)

- 『예수님과 걷는 길 4편, 복음의 능력』 (*Journey With Jesus Four, The Power of the Gospel*)

- 『용서가 낳은 치유의 은혜』 (*Tornadoes, Grief, Loss Trauma, and PTSD: Tornadoes, Lessons and Teachings—The TLT Model for Healing*)

About The Illustrator

-Holly Weipz-

Holly Weipz, a resident of Brighton Colorado, is a participant in the City of Brighton's Artist on Eye of Art Program. She is a member of St. Augustine Catholic Church and enjoys drawing and painting.

About The Illustrator

-Mario Muñoz-

"I was listening to Chaplain McDonald during a Chaplain's Worship Service. She was praying about our relationship with God. I immediately felt compelled to create illustrations for her, all the while having no knowledge of *Journey With Jesus Two* or its contents. When I finally had the awesome opportunity to read the book, it transformed my life. I now understand the great need for listening to and obeying God. *Journey With Jesus Two* is certain to drive home the importance of listening to what God wants to tell you!"
—Mario Muñoz

About The Illustrator

-Anthony Perez-

Anthony Perez is a father, graphic designer, poet and painter. He shows his work in Colorado galleries and in the historic Westminster Arts District of which he is also designer of their logo. He also illustrates and has been published in various other context.

Anthony /Atus explains...

"I have been an artist all of my life. I am blessed to be able to follow the path the Lord Jesus has showed me and to use my talents to glorify His name, especially behind these walls. Roman 12:21 explains my goals. Chaplain McDonald's books are a true blessing. To have the opportunity to work on the illustrations of *Journey With Jesuf Four* with her for the glory of Jesus Christ is an answered prayer. Halleluiah."

Anthony "Atus" Perez.
Atuscadabo.wix.com/atuscadabra

"For all have sinned and fall short of the glory of God, and are justified freely by his grace through the redemption that came by Christ Jesus." (Romans 3:23)

"For God so loved the world that he gave his one and only Son, that whoever believes in him shall not perish but have eternal life." (John 3:16)

"Therefore, there is now no condemnation for those who are in Christ Jesus, because through Christ Jesus the law of the Spirit of life set me free from the law of sin and death." (Romans 8:1-2)

"He who has an ear, let him hear what the Spirit says to the churches. To him who overcomes, I will give the right to eat from the tree of life, which is in the paradise of God." (Revelation 2:7)

"To him who overcomes and does my will to the end, I will give authority over the nations." (Revelation 2:26)

"They overcame him by the blood of the Lamb and by the word of their testimony." (Revelation 12:11a)

"Then I saw a new heaven and a new earth, for the first heaven and the first earth had passed away, and there was no longer any sea. I saw the Holy City, the new Jerusalem, coming down out of heaven from God, prepared as a bride beautifully dressed for her husband. And I heard a loud voice from the throne saying, 'Now the dwelling of God is with men, and he will live with them. They will be his people, and God himself will be with them and be their God. He will wipe every tear from their eyes. There will be no more death or mourning or crying or pain, for the old order of things has passed away.' He who was seated on the throne said, 'I am making everything new!' Then he said, 'Write this down, for these words are trustworthy and true.' He said to me: 'It is done. I am the Alpha and the Omega, the Beginning and the End. To him who is thirsty I will give to drink without cost from the spring of the water of life. He who overcomes will inherit all this, and I will be his God and he will be my son.'" (Revelation 21:1-7)

"I planted the seed, Apollos watered it, but God made it grow. So neither he who plants nor he who waters is anything, but only God, who makes things grow. The man who plants and the man who waters have one purpose, and each will be rewarded according to his own labor. For we are God's fellow workers; you are God's field, God's building." (1 Corinthians 3:6-9)